# The Phenomena of Awa

**What is awareness? How is dreaming different from ordinary awareness? What does mathematics have to do with awareness? Are different kinds of awareness related?**

'Awareness' is commonly spoken of as 'mind, soul, spirit, consciousness, the unconscious, psyche, imagination, self, and other.' *The Phenomena of Awareness* is a study of awareness as it is directly experienced. From the start, Cecile T. Tougas engages the reader in reflective notice of awareness as it appears from moment to moment in a variety of ways. The book draws us in and asks us to focus on the flow of phenomena in living experience, not as a theoretical construct, nor an image, nor a biochemical product, but instead as phases, moments, or parts that cannot exist without one another. Tougas shows how these parts exist in mutual dependence as a continuum of awareness, as the flow of lived time, and how noticing time deepens psychological self-understanding and understanding of another.

*The Phenomena of Awareness* is divided into four parts:

- Seeking and noticing awareness
- Observing and understanding the flow of phenomena
- Distinguishing intentional acts
- Work in progress.

Drawing on the work of E. Husserl, G. Cantor, and C. G. Jung, this book is an original synthesis of phenomenology, mathematics, and psychology that explores awareness and the concept 'transfinite number.' This book will be of interest to analytical psychologists, philosophers, mathematicians, feminist scholars, humanities teachers, and students.

**Cecile T. Tougas** teaches Latin at the North Carolina School of Science and Mathematics, Durham. She taught philosophy at the University of Southern Maine and the University of Massachusetts Lowell.

# The Phenomena of Awareness

Husserl, Cantor, Jung

Cecile T. Tougas

 Routledge
Taylor & Francis Group

LONDON AND NEW YORK

First published 2013 by Routledge
27 Church Road, Hove, East Sussex BN3 2FA

Simultaneously published in the USA and Canada
by Routledge
711 Third Avenue, New York NY 10017

*Routledge is an imprint of the Taylor & Francis Group, an informa
business*

*British Library Cataloguing in Publication Data*
A catalogue record for this book is available from the British
Library

*Library of Congress Cataloging in Publication Data*

Tougas, Cecile T. (Cécile Thérèse), 1947-
The phenomena of awareness : Husserl, Cantor, Jung / Cecile T.
Tougas.
p. cm.
1. Awareness. 2. Consciousness. 3. Title.
BF321.T74 2012
128'.3--dc23
2012000273

ISBN: 978-0-415-68590-0 (hbk)
ISBN: 978-0-415-68591-7 (pbk)
ISBN: 978-0-203-10538-2 (ebk)

Typeset in Times by Fakenham Prepress Solutions, Fakenham,
Norfolk NR21 8NN

MIX
Paper from
responsible sources
FSC www.fsc.org FSC® C004839

Printed and bound in Great Britain by
TJ International Ltd, Padstow, Cornwall

# Contents

# Acknowledgements

I thank the John Anson Kittredge Fund, Cambridge, Massachusetts, for a fellowship in 1994 that enabled me to have a sabbatical year for writing.

I am very grateful to William Willeford whose reading of my manuscript at various stages led to invaluable discussion of matters small and large.

I thank Kathryn H. Whalen for programming the bibliography, aligning the references, and reading the book.

I also thank ICS Publications for permission to quote material written by Edith Stein:
From *On the Problem of Empathy* by Edith Stein translated by Waltraut Stein, Ph.D. Copyright © 1989 by Washington Province of Discalced Carmelites ICS Publications 2131 Lincoln Road, N.E. Washington, DC 20002–1199 U.S.A. (www.icspublications.org)

From *Self-Portrait in Letters* translated by Josephine Koeppel, O.C.D. Copyright © 1993 Washington Province of Discalced Carmelites ICS Publications 2131 Lincoln Road, N.E. Washington, DC 20002–1199 (www.icspublications.org)

From *Life in a Jewish Family* translated by Josephine Koeppel, O.C.D. Copyright © 1986 by Washington Province of Discalced Carmelites ICS Publications 2131 Lincoln Road, N.E. Washington, DC 20002–1199 U.S.A. (www.icspublications.org)

I also thank Houghton Mifflin Harcourt Publishing Company for permission to quote a poem:
"Anterooms" from *ANTEROOMS: New Poems and Translations* by Richard Wilbur. Copyright © 2010 by Richard Wilbur. Reprinted by permission of Houghton Mifflin Harcourt Publishing Company. All rights reserved.

I also thank Princeton University Press for permission to quote lines from the Upanishads found in:
Radhakrishnan, Sarvepalli and Charles A. Moore: *A Source Book in Indian Philosophy*; © 1957 Princeton University Press, Renewed 1985. Reprinted by permission of Princeton University Press.

And I thank Oxford University Press for permission to quote these lines from the Upanishads as originally published in:
Hume, R. E.: *The Thirteen Principal Upanishads,* 2nd ed. rev.; © 1931 Oxford University Press. Reprinted by permission of Oxford University Press.

With kind permission from Springer Science+Business Media B.V., I gratefully use a diagram by Edmund Husserl from A, First Part, Second section (*Analyse des Zeitbewusstseins*), paragraph 10 (*Die Kontinua der Ablaufsphänomene.—Das Diagramm der Zeit*), page 28 of:
*Husserliana 10: Zur Phänomenologie des inneren Zeitbewusstseins (1893–1917).* [The Phenomenology of internal time-consciousness (1893–1917).] Edmund Husserl. Edited by Rudolf Boehm. The Hague, Netherlands: Martinus Nijhoff, 1969. © 1969 by Martinus Nijhoff, The Hague, Netherlands; All rights reserved, including the right to translate or to reproduce this book or parts thereof in any form.

# Introduction

This book is a study of awareness as temporal flux in various kinds of intentional activities. It is based on the work of Edmund Husserl (1859–1938), founder of contemporary phenomenology. Husserl remains little-known, while Heidegger, Merleau-Ponty, Sartre, Derrida, and others inspired by Husserl are better known. But his original phenomenological view is needed today, particularly in psychological discussions of self and other, and consciousness and the unconscious. Such a view examines awareness, describes it, and makes distinctions in it that psychologists have often passed over but will be glad to discover. Unlike many books on Husserl, and even many introductions, this book shows in a living way the value of his central insights and their importance for psychological self-understanding and understanding of another.

I begin by giving examples of being drawn to notice awareness in a variety of ways. I was moved by dreams; Socrates was attracted to the mind and Ideas; Husserl was drawn to repeatedly notice phenomena in temporal flux; Jung was pulled by images in the unconscious; Edith Stein left home to follow philosophical spirit; Camus missed something and cried out in the dark; William James, Brentano, Husserl, and Freud were compelled to study intentionality without quite knowing what it was. Thus, the first part of this book makes it evident that awareness is an interest, an attraction, a spontaneous seeking after meaning, and a tending toward the fulfillment of that meaning in some kind of perception of the meant as present in some way. We tend towards something significant and long to have it before us. Sometimes the "something" is awareness itself.

In this book, "awareness" is the something that is sought. It is the meant object that needs to be perceived more fully, the other that is nevertheless subjectively lived. The spontaneous tending of awareness has been called "intentionality" and it occurs in a variety of ways which are sometimes simultaneous. For example, expecting, perceiving, and remembering are simultaneous intentional activities that make up our experience. Through them there is a flow of appearances or "phenomena" by which meant objects appear, as expected, perceived, and remembered. Meant objects include, for example, trees, songs, feelings, numbers, the Idea of "Equal," another person, another person's feeling, one's intentional acts, and the flow of appearances itself.

We can turn our attention repeatedly to study intentionality and the flow of phenomena which come to be present because expecting is open to the future, memory is retaining the past in the now moment, and memory continues to hold the widening past in each new moment (as past, then as farther past, then as even farther past, and so on). The present moment of perceiving, continually new, is inseparable from the expecting and the retaining. It actually holds much, and, implicitly, much more. It can be understood as "transfinite," as a continuing whole, just as each integer or whole counting number (1, 2, 3 …) is transfinite insofar as it contains the infinite series of numbers before it. Each new present moment contains infinite series of past moments, most of which are not seen well or counted specifically. "Transfinite" is a term for the infinite as clarified by Georg Cantor, a colleague of Husserl. In this book I explain the concept of "transfinite" in a beginning way in order to appreciate the significance of the present moment of awareness.

It is time for the present moment to be noticed as transfinite. Old ways of understanding an infinite series as one successive line are inadequate for even just glimpsing the present moment of awareness in its fullness and mystery. Leibniz, Cantor, and Husserl had a sense of the transfinite and through it were able to observe how an individual part of the continuum of awareness has a one-to-one correspondence with the whole, and how the whole exists in the individual part. Jung had some sense of the reciprocal correspondence of part and whole. With an understanding of the present moment as merely a point in one successive series or horizontal line, though, an individual part does not have a one-to-one correspondence (or "equivalence") to its whole. For, as I show in the book, only with infinite series does a part have equivalence (not equality) to its whole. Since the present moment and its memory are doubly continuous, successively in two lines perpendicular to each other, each moment holds an infinite series or vertical line of past moments. In the second part of the book I spend much time explaining the relation of these two "lines" in time. The present of awareness intends the future and retains the past anew at each new moment. It is a continuous transfinite whole that has parts that are equivalent to it. I spend three chapters paying attention to this complexity and attempting to describe it. It is time that Cantor's concept of the transfinite be described outside of high school mathematics textbooks and used in the study of awareness. We have long counted time. Counting time with a transfinite number is now possible and is necessary for a study of awareness.

Awareness as a flow of phenomena or appearances is spontaneously constituted in the simultaneous intentional activities of expecting the future, perceiving the present, and remembering the past. The three are distinct yet inseparable. One cannot exist without the other two. Moreover, they all depend on the spontaneous arising of a new moment that makes awareness possible in the first place.

Awareness is not a concrete object made of physical parts. Rather, it is a relative whole constituted by distinct parts that are inseparable from one another. It is a continuum that is part of a continuum and that has continua as parts. Noticing such continuity is mind-boggling. But at least such noticing tends to prevent the mistake of assuming that awareness is just like the many concrete things it makes present. In the second part of this book, I make repeated attempts, as Husserl did, to notice and describe aspects of awareness.

The third part of the book provides descriptions of some intentional activities. I quote lines and paragraphs from Edith Stein's autobiography because they show remembering and feeling in her living and they evoke a response in us. I also bring to light an intentionality that is far too little noticed: expectation or tending toward the future. It is a tending toward the non-yet, the about-to-be, the can-be, and the ought-to-be as necessarily connected to what is and what was. Emphasizing the baby of the future is its job.

The study of awareness also makes it clear that dreams are not just images. Indeed, they are phenomena of their own kind. Like empathy as an act of knowing the feeling of another as other, dreaming is first of all an act in which something other than itself is genuinely present. Sensation is not the only kind of perceptive intentionality, for existence is not only seen, heard, touched, tasted, or smelled, but is also felt, remembered, and dreamed. A dream is not reducible to fantasy or image even though it may represent much through symbols or images. A dream gives the presence of some objectivity. We live with the ones we dream about, even though we cannot explain their existence and their presence to us.

Near the end of his life, after he had been silenced in Germany, Husserl said outright before a crowd in Vienna: "Our surrounding world is a work of spirit, in us and our historical life." (Husserl 1977a: 24–5) Without having heard, met, or studied Husserl, Jung made a similar affirmation and referred specifically to Schopenhauer's view of intentionality as ground, cause, and energy. Galaxies, nebulae, ancient times, and we ourselves are linked back to a core, to what we cannot exist without: the work of spirit that underlies each moment of awareness and intends the phenomena we live.

Accordingly, in the last part of the book I seek out the work of spirit as in progress today. Mutual personal presence is crucial in analytical psychology and I affirm it, especially in regard to a currently popular assumption that appearances are merely images. Self and other, in their many ways of appearing to and for one another, are experienced as present, living, and real; they are not mere representations of fantasy. Analysis is not a small room in which images are projected.

Another form of mutual presence is the experience a woman has with a part of herself that is other insofar as it is experienced as masculine. Jung was attentive to such experience and called the masculine aspect of a woman "animus," while calling the feminine aspect of a man "anima." I give examples and describe ways in which the other is given in such experience.

In this book, I make deliberate specific repetitions. Repetition is an ancient classical rhetorical device of style and it is called "anaphora." Søren Kierkegaard wrote a book called *Repetition*. He maintained that the form of expression must reduplicate the content. How a thing is said must reflect what is being said. For consistency, then, he should have called the book *Repetition Repetition*. But that title is boring. In this book, I make repetitions that should not be boring because they have an important purpose: to emphasize connections in parts of a whole. In this way I use another ancient classical rhetorical device of style that is called "ring composition."

Ring composition is the putting together of parts in a certain order. Typically the order is ABCDE in beginning, then a crisis or climax in the middle, and then an EDCBA order in ending. The parts circle back around the center like rings. After the crisis or climax in the middle, however, each part returns as remembered and as changed. While I do not repeat parts in the exact order of EDCBA, I do bring important parts back, as remembered with added significance in relation to the book's central theme, subjectivity.

I did not explicitly plan to use ring composition when I started writing this book twenty years ago. In fact, I noticed its use only recently while revising the last chapters. It is evident to me now that an implicit intent was and is at work in the writing.

Part of this intent in writing has been the desire to participate in the illuminating recent discussion of basic Jungian concepts, especially that discussion which has, without protest, been called "anti-essentialist." In this book, with Aristotle, Leibniz, Husserl, and Cantor, I affirm the importance of understanding "essence" as a concept, a limit of what a thing is. An example of "essence" is the concept "number," which we mean whenever we count, and without which we cannot count. Indeed, the meaning of money, clocks, and computers depends on the essence "number." This book insists on a wider discussion of "essence" as non-material yet as crucial to daily experience.

# Part I

# Seeking and noticing awareness

# Chapter 1

# Medieval metaphysics

When I was young and growing up, I lived in what today can be called a medieval metaphysical world. For me as a child, there was no questioning: I lived in an immortal soul and everyone else did as well. Moreover, each person had something to do for which he or she was responsible, as each was eternally significant. Both the soul and the body were sustained at every moment by God. My great-grandparents who had died still existed somehow in spirit, though to me that meant something that was also body. We could associate with them in prayer; my mother's mother prayed every day for a year after her mother died, for her soul to pass through purgatory. There was indeed a spiritual world. Members of my family, historical figures, and saints lived there. The unborn were rather vague and lived in a grey area.

After I stopped speaking French as a primary language, spoke English instead, and left Catholic school, the sense of the immortal soul and the spiritual world became less vivid but was still present. I found Darwin very exciting to read, for I was also reading Pierre Teilhard de Chardin, a French Jesuit who interpreted evolution as an emergence from God, a deployment and intensification of self-consciousness through matter towards its Alpha and Omega. I studied Immanuel Kant's *Critique of Pure Reason* and knew as C. G. Jung did that that critique could never be reduced to "the harmonious interplay of the drives of hunger, love, and power." (Jung 1969: 341) Rather, Kant's Critiques, especially his *Critique of Practical Reason*, reaffirmed in me the hope in spirit as "something" in and for itself, as having its own distinct character, not exactly as self-contained but more as communing with the rest of our world. I felt that each person I knew, or knew of, was an autonomous individual soul, despite whatever else they were.

My medieval metaphysical perspective, however, got pushed to the background of my attention as divorce, work, and child-raising came to demand more and more of my energy. I had to learn the ways of the modern world through the daily rigors of my jobs. I had to accept the independent attitudes of my children as they were growing up and then living on their own. Soul and spirit were present to me then mostly in dreams. For many years after his death, the children's father appeared in my dreams, and we both changed over the years. I recorded my dreams whether big or small, and I participated in Jungian analysis.

The presence of a dead person in a dream as existing right before me and with me seemed natural. It was more than imaginary: it was phenomenal and spiritual. Someone was appearing as "phenomenon" or "given in some kind of experience." His presence grabbed my spirit by a feeling that I could not deny. I knew when I awoke that I had been dreaming. But I also knew that reality has many aspects. Sounds and colors are not the only things that appear. Through them something inescapable was there in the dream, not merely imagined or fantasized. It was much more than anything material. It was what I had experienced as a child and called "spiritual." It was something of its own kind appearing in dream color, sound, and touch. I could not reduce it to material processes in the brain. Nor was I able to convince myself that what was present was not actually existent. I was not attracted by the modern presumption that each person can construct his or her own reality. Objectivity hit me in dreams, taught me, and made demands on me. I could not control my dreams any more than I could control my workplace or my children.

I did not find support for my dream experience in science, however, as the scientific attitude withholds assent from a metaphysical assertion of the existence of spirit or soul. Instead, it gives assent to the presupposition that the world is material, causal, and physical—a presupposition that is no less metaphysical, inasmuch as it affirms something about a whole that is only partially experienced. Most scientists, and many people of our age, nevertheless assume that spatial and temporal reality exists on its own apart from experiencing subjectivity, as an objective reality without value and feeling. Moreover, they believe that science is the only kind of genuine knowledge and that scientific method is the only sure way to such knowledge. In their view, literature, art, and society express aspects of human beings that are "subjective"—arbitrary, relative, unreliable—rather than objective, scientific, and true. Accordingly, spirit and soul as transcendent and immaterial are considered to be fantasies or illusions, stripped of any binding objectivity, neither true nor necessary. "Freedom to choose" thus comes to mean diversity as a wide menu of equally possible options, rather than anxiety as a fear and trembling of personal responsibility in the face of something transcendent. Among such viewpoints I did not find support for my dream experience.

Dreams in the background of my attention nevertheless held out against the modern, scientific, and postmodern world. Soul and spirit did not behave as though they were medieval and outdated; rather, they acted as though they belonged in existence, just like the trees outside the window and the sun setting in the evening. I found words to begin to express them by studying and practicing the phenomenological philosophy of Edmund Husserl (1859–1938) who repeatedly turned his attention to consciousness and described it in words as a stream of appearances or the phenomena of awareness. The phenomena of awareness as such do not belong to any one person and can be noticed by anyone.

In his writing, Husserl provides a method, distinct from the scientific method, for noticing the phenomena of awareness and so for attaining genuine knowledge about subjectivity as living awareness. In his "phenomenological method," which he practiced and described for many years, he repeatedly turned his attention to the flow of subjective experience. As a child, I had felt this vital flow of life as spirit or soul. Through direct notice of experience while it is happening, experience becomes evident as a lived stream of consciousness that is not reducible to biochemical processes posited as occurring in a brain. The complex flux of perception, memory, feeling, and other intentional activities—such as dreaming—is thus accepted as its own kind of objectivity, not material but rather "intentional" or "tending toward meaning." Husserl repeatedly turned his attention to the stream of appearances, the phenomena of awareness, in which we and the world are intentionally—meaningfully—present to ourselves in a wide variety of ways. While it is lived individually, the stream does not belong to just one person; it is available for notice by anyone, just as a tree or a sunset is able to be noticed in a wide variety of ways. This book describes ways in which to notice the phenomena of awareness, first of all through missing it and seeking it; then through observing and understanding its flow; and then through distinguishing various modes of intentional awareness. In the last section I speak about the study of awareness as a work in progress.

This book is an expression not only of observing and understanding, but also of feeling, remembering, hoping, imagining, hearing, and other acts of meaning that bring something before us. I tell how hearing a sound as Husserl and Saint Augustine heard it changed my life. I relate how Edith Stein left home and went to Göttingen to study with Husserl; as I quote parts of her autobiography, I reflect on the significance of her life as she is remembering and feeling its significance. I describe Camus in the dread and desert world of night that he lived in as speaker for the anxiety of the twentieth century. Referring to Husserl and Cantor, I understand the flow of awareness as a transfinite continuity that is double because it is continually held in spontaneous memory. With Husserl, Leibniz, Jung, and Marie-Louise von Franz in mind, I take note of horizons of awareness. Throughout the book I imagine and hope that the reader is performing similar intentional activities, and, moreover, is noticing them, making distinctions about them, and appreciating them with me.

# Chapter 2

# The Equal

One way in which to notice the spiritual world is to glimpse it as the life of mind or intelligence. Ancient Greek philosophers, and Plato in particular, made it a practice to seek "Ideas" or *eide*, the forms, shapes, or essences of existing objects. But it is difficult today even to imagine a time long ago when thinkers sought and tried to live in the presence of Ideas, such as the Just, the Good, or the Equal.

To provoke my students into reflection, I ask them to consider the number 3. Does it exist? Look at it. Where is it? It is not in space. It exists in the continuum between 2 and 4. Is it still there? They nod. I add that in different languages and various ways of counting, what we call "3" has other names: *trois,* III, *tres, drei,* "10" in the binary system. Yet these words name the same entity: only the one number, 3. Do not mathematicians in Russia see the same number that we do here? $3 = 3$. Students begin to see that the number we see is indeed the same, despite our different instances of experiencing it and our various ways of naming it.

Then I ask them to consider =. Could anyone do any mathematics, even simple arithmetic, without knowing what = or "equal" is? No, they say readily. Look at "equal." Is your "equal" different from his, hers, or mine? Then the students say, "Oh, yes; each one of us has his or her own 'equal'. For each has a different view of it; we live in a democracy and are entitled to our own views." They do not think that there is only one = the way there is only one 3. I then ask them, is your perspective or active viewing of "equal" distinct from the "equal" you are viewing? But they think that only their perspectives exist. They seem to think that they make up or construct what "equal" is. So I ask, does each of you have an "equal" that is different from the "equal" of the others? Yes, they say. So then, your "equal" is not equal to the "equal" of the others? They nod. Then what kind of "equal" is that? That is not a very good "equal," is it, if all its instances are unequal to one another? Look further. For you to know that your "equal" is not equal to that of the others, you have to know what "equal" means as the Equal, the way 3 is the Three. There is only one Equal.

The students are stunned, puzzled, and silent. It seems that they had never noticed the existence of the Equal, as existing objectively as itself, like 3 and other numbers. Unlike many mathematicians who know the Equal exists and there is only one 3, the students believed that they had been taught what = or "equal" means, the way they had learned that Paris is the capital of France. They had assumed that knowledge of "equal" came from outside their minds as they were learning the meaning of the word. They had not recognized that the Equal exists immaterially as its own kind of object.

I persist and ask, how can you know what things are equal, or what "equal" means, without already having some sense of the Equal as an Idea, against which and by which you are able to recognize instances of equals? If you do not have that sense of Equal to begin with, no one can explain to you what equalities and inequalities are, no matter how many instances of them they may put before you. Ideas, such as 3 and =, exist non-spatially, in an implicit abundance of mind or soul, as a basis for explicit, focused knowing.

This is a surprise. My students are accustomed to thinking of mental life as a closed-off private sphere of uniquely individual experiences. They say: "No one else can know my intentions and feelings, as no one is precisely me; each person is different from all the others." It is shocking for them to glimpse an Idea or Ideal form, like the Equal or the Just, as present for the mind in quite a non-private way, inasmuch as it is the same for all, implicitly grasped as in a continuum. While students often talk on their cell phones and communicate by laptop with people quite far away, they do not reflect and notice that such presence to one another presupposes that their minds are already interconnected in a community that is as vast as the continuum of number in which one number is what it is only in relation to all the others.

The mind is not "internal" like a box, a car, or a house. It is not spatial and so it is not "in" or "out." By observing a number or an Ideal form such as the Equal, we can begin to get a sense of the genuine existence of actual objects that are immaterial, intelligent, or spiritual. In this way we can make an approach to studying the phenomena of awareness, which do not exist the way boxes, cars, and houses do. Rather, the appearances of awareness exist as a temporal flux, an immaterial flowing that makes objectivity—whether numbers, *eide*, or spatial things—present and that is nevertheless inseparable from what it makes present.

# Chapter 3

# Jung's "images" and Husserl's "phenomena"

Edmund Husserl and C. G. Jung noticed phenomena of awareness. While Husserl called them "phenomena" or "appearances," Jung called them "images," but both terms refer to whatever is before any kind of awareness. There are grounds for asserting that "image" in Jung is what "phenomenon" is in Husserl. If so, "the psychological standpoint" for Jung coincides with what might be called "the phenomenological standpoint" for Husserl. Jung writes:

> I do not contest the relative validity either of the realistic standpoint, the *esse in re* [being in the thing], or of the idealistic standpoint, the *esse in intellectu solo* [being in the intellect alone]; I would only like to unite these extreme opposites by an *esse in anima* [being in the soul], which is the psychological standpoint. We live immediately only in the world of images.
>
> (Jung 1969: 327–8)

Jung did not affirm that existence is merely *esse in re*, the material reality of the world. Yet he did not affirm that existence is merely *esse in intellectu solo*, the ideal actuality of intellects. In a fuller way, he affirmed the existence of both as *esse in anima*, the being in the soul. Ancient Greek philosophers saw this continuum as the whole of nature and number. Like them, Jung saw that we live immediately only in this fundamental being. Unfortunately, however, like many modern thinkers, and David Hume in particular, Jung's English translators called our immediate experience "image" or "idea" rather than "appearance" or "phenomenon." The difficulty is that images and ideas are representations of things beyond them, whereas immediate experience is the presence of something as given "right here."

Experience is a living flow in which things are given as immediately present, not merely as represented. I look at a tree and see it is before me as I live the experience of seeing it; it is present, not merely represented; I have an appearance or "phenomenon" of the tree, not just a representational picture, image, or idea of it. Even though many aspects of the tree are not directly present to me, the objective tree is nonetheless inseparable from its moments of appearing to me as existing beyond me. The real tree is the experienced one, which is not somehow twenty feet away from itself as an "image in my brain." So it is more accurate to name what we experience immediately as "moments of appearance" or "presenting phenomena," rather than "images" or "ideas."

Jung sensed this problem, as his English translator and editor at the time was using the words "image" and "idea" for the German word *Vorstellung*, which means "presentation" even as it also means "representation." In a letter of 15 August 1958 to R. F. C. Hull, his English translator, Jung found "indeed a serious trouble" in the English rendering of the German word *Idee* as "idea," when the German word *Vorstellung* is also translated as "idea" or "image." (Jung n.d.: 460)

Translating both *Idee* and *Vorstellung* as "idea" or "image" is indeed troublesome, as Jung said. For *Vorstellung* means whatever is given as present to awareness, whereas *Idee* can refer to *eidos* in the original Platonic sense, an essence such as the Equal or Three, or it can refer to Kant's specific use of the term, which I will soon explain. *Idee* has, according to Jung, "retained the original meaning of a transcendental *eidos*, respectively of *eidolon*, when it becomes manifest .... Where I speak of '*Idee*,' it always means something similar to Kant and Plato." (Jung n.d.: 460) But when translators render both *Idee* and *Vorstellung* as the same, the result is not only that the very special sense of *Idee* is lost, but also that "image" that merely represents reality takes the place of "appearance" that presents reality. Indeed, *Vorstellung* as whatever comes before awareness has a wide meaning that includes both presenting appearance and representing image. But when it is translated merely as "image," a reader is apt to think that Jung believes we have only "images in the brain" which represent a reality separate from them, with the result that we do not have access to reality as actually present to us. When Jung speaks of *esse in anima* or the being of the soul, however, it is evident that he recognizes the existence of a fundamental being through which reality is given to us as actual in a variety of ways. He calls it "soul."

Translators aside, Jung himself could have been clearer about these distinctions and could have been more persistent in demanding corrections. While he did recognize that we live immediately only in the fundamental being of the soul, he did not explain that what Kant means by the German term *Idee* is not exactly what Plato means by the Greek term *eidos*. For Plato, each thing participates in an *eidos* which exists beyond the thing and makes the thing be what it is. For Kant, an *Idee* is a pure a priori concept of the understanding and it exceeds the conditions of the possibility of our experience; as Kant indicates in A334–5/ B391–2, "the world" is the cosmological *Idee*, "the soul" is the psychological *Idee,* and "God" is the theological *Idee*. (Kant 1963: 323) Moreover, *Idee* comes under the heading of *Vorstellung,* as one of its kinds.

*Vorstellung* as a whole refers to whatever we have before us as appearing in awareness. Kant uses the term in *The Critique of Pure Reason*, A319–320/ B376–377, as a heading for various kinds of "appearance" in general. (Kant 1963: 314) Starting with sensate experience as a kind of *Vorstellung*, Kant then distinguishes in it concepts as aspects of experience that are not perceived by our senses but rather are thought by our understanding.

A concept can be empirical, like the concept "red," which is not a seen red but is rather a general thought which grasps together whatever is seen as red. Or, a concept can be nonempirical or pure, like the concept "extension" which itself is not extended but is rather a general thought which grasps together whatever is experienced as extended. Obviously, then, sensations and concepts are distinct, even as they have relations of dependence among them. For example, color and visual extension cannot exist without each other, and so they are said to be recip- rocally non-independent. Kant persistently affirmed that our sense experience as a whole is constituted by both sensations and concepts.

Moreover, a pure concept can be a posteriori, known from experience, like the concept of triangle, which is known by attention and reflection on what is given in sense experience. Or, a pure concept can be a priori, known as a condition for the possibility of experience, like a concept of quantity, which is known not only by attention and reflection on what is given in sense experience but is also recog- nized as constitutive of experience, as necessary for its existence. Distinguishing between one and two is fundamental to the experience of the world insofar as the world is more than one thing. Concepts of quantity and other pure a priori concepts of the understanding exist as fundamentally forming our sensate experience, which itself has space and time as its own a priori, as the pure forms of our sensibility.

These forming aspects of our experience can be recognized. They are condi- tions for the possibility of experience; the various kinds of things that actually do appear to us could not appear to us without them. They are aspects of *Vorstellung* as fundamental, constitutive, or "transcendental." But there is yet another kind of *Vorstellung: Idee* or Idea which is a pure a priori concept of the understanding which is not only transcendental or fundamental to experience, but is also trans- cendent or beyond experience. The world as a whole, the soul in its depth, and God as infinite creator cannot be understood adequately, nor can they be perceived sensately. They are given as concepts that exceed our experience, even as they are thought necessarily as foundation for subjective experience of the world.

Thus, *Vorstellung* includes not only the presentation of what is present directly but also includes the representation of what is present indirectly. For many years, however, *Vorstellung* has been translated deficiently as "representation," although more recently it is sometimes translated as "presentation."

Kant beseeched "those who have the interests of philosophy at heart" that "they be careful to preserve the expression 'idea' [*Idee*] in its original meaning," and not use it to indicate any and every kind of *Vorstellung*. (Kant 1963: 314) Jung shared Kant's concern but not did not make the careful distinctions among the kinds of *Vorstellung* that Kant had made. Both would have welcomed Husserl's use of the term "appearance" or "phenomenon" to speak in general of whatever is before consciousness. For Husserl recognized not only how important it is to make distinctions but also how important it is to see that living experience is foremost an appearing of something present; it is not merely a representation or image of something beyond that is not directly present.

Agreeing with Kant, Jung affirmed that an *Idee* should keep its name in order to avoid confusion with *Vorstellung* as a name for appearance in general. But, not acting as Kant had, Jung failed to specify to his audience the distinct kinds of *Vorstellung* important to Kant. As it is, we often find in Jung's writing the word "image," not to mention the word "archetype" meant as an Idea or *Idee*, without a clarification of *Vorstellung* as both presentation and representation, and as including *Idee* under its heading as both transcendental and transcendent to experience. Indeed, there are "imaginal psychologists," who claim to be following Jung when they assume that experience is imaginal and that psyche is fantasy, and I will address these assumptions in Chapter 18.

Jung could have saved both his translators and his readers much trouble by writing a few paragraphs like the preceding ones about Kant and *Vorstellung*. Moreover, he could have replaced the sentence "We live immediately only in the world of images" with "We live immediately only in the world of phenomena or appearances." For we live in our experience as a flux of awareness that gives us the presence of whatever is appearing, as *esse in anima*, as being in the soul—as being in the abundance of it all, the continuum, the whole of nature and number. Reality lives in our living of it—not merely as *re*, thing, nor as *intellectu*, intellect, but as *anima*, soul, as continual flow of experience which is a felt intentional ("tending toward meaning") activity, reducible to neither material body nor abstract intellect. Soul, far from being an ancient or medieval relic, is experienced as the life of meaning by which anything at all appears as present to anyone, in a variety of ways. Recognizing the being in the soul is thus attaining "the psychological standpoint" as a philosophical attitude.

For Husserl, what might be called "the phenomenological standpoint" is the same way of observing. Husserl found it self-evident that we need to begin with whatever is given to us, to observe it repeatedly as it presents itself, and to accept it as genuinely present within the limits of its being present. He explicitly formulates this way of coming to knowledge as "the principle of all principles":

> ... *every primordial dator Intuition* is *a source of authority (Rechtsquelle) for knowledge* ... *whatever presents itself in "intuition" in primordial form* (as it were in its bodily reality), *is simply to be accepted as it gives itself out to be, though only within the limits in which it then presents itself.*
> (Husserl 1958: 92, emphasis in original)

By the term "intuition," Husserl means a beholding of anything at all, according to the meaning of the Latin word *intueor*, "look at, watch; contemplate, consider; admire." (Kidd 1961: 179) Intuition is not only the observing of whatever is present, but is also the basic activity specific to phenomenology as the practice of watching phenomena or appearances to awareness. Insofar as the term "dator" means "giving" and "primordial" means "of the first order" or "original," then, a "primordial dator Intuition" is a noticing that gives something originally, as itself present, not merely as represented. Such intuiting is a source of authority for knowledge: it has to be. It is evident that we have to start with what is evident; the first evidence has to be self-evident. We proceed and accept whatever is given as itself present, as itself (be it a tree, a number, a person—anything at all in the widest sense of "thing"), though only within the limits of its being given as present. We watch whatever appears and how it appears, and we accept it as an aspect of reality within the limits of its appearing. We notice attentively, observe repeatedly, make distinctions, and describe carefully.

Thus, to be phenomenological, we need to turn our attention to actual phenomena of awareness. Such attentiveness or intuition, the direct noticing of what is present to some mode of awareness, is the basic activity of phenomenological practice. It is a shift of attention, a turning to contemplate and watch explicitly the living awareness that is happening as it is happening. It is not only the concrete hearing of music, the compassionate remembering of a friend, or the abstract seeing of the angles in a triangle, but at the same time is also the noticing of the hearing, the remembering, or the seeing as intentional ("tending towards meaning") activities in a stream of experiencing awareness whose appearances make both the "things" (in the widest sense of the word "thing") and the intentional activities present. We notice that the music and the intentional activity of hearing are distinct yet inseparable. In Chapter 10 we will pay special attention to the stream or flux of awareness as time.

There is an intentional flux of awareness present during moments of perceiving and attention in general; often the flux is not itself noticed. Nevertheless, we can repeatedly turn our attention to this flux, aiming to glimpse what is mostly "in the background" of our notice. When we deliberately sustain our intuiting of appearing awareness itself (confirming once again that it is indeed a flow, flux, stream—known, noticed again from moment to moment), we are practicing phenomenology. It is repeated effort to observe what Jung called *esse in anima*, the being of soul, the abundant continuum in which self and world are experienced as genuinely themselves. Thus, Jung and Husserl had at least one common aim: to watch the soul streaming and accept the reality it gives.

# Chapter 4

# Edith Stein and Husserl in Göttingen

Another way to approach the study of the phenomena of awareness is to pay attention to some recorded experiences of early phenomenologists as they were working with one another. It is informative to reflect on Edith Stein's account of the time when she came to study with Husserl. Getting a sense of what drew her to Husserl, and what drew Husserl to study awareness, can provide us with a sense of phenomenology as a lived study.

Stein wrote in her autobiography:

> Neither striking nor overwhelming, his external appearance was rather of an elegant professorial type. His height was average; his bearing, dignified; his head, handsome and impressive. His speech at once betrayed his Austrian birth: he came from Moravia and had studied in Vienna. His serene amiability also had something of old Vienna about it. He had just completed his fifty-fourth year.
>
> (Stein 1986: 249)

With these words from her autobiography, *Life in a Jewish Family 1891–1916*, first published in English in 1986, Edith Stein describes how she saw Husserl for the first time in the spring of 1913. She had been struck by him in advance, moved and drawn by his *Logical Investigations*, published in 1900. During the Christmas break from the University of Breslau in 1912, she had spent her days in a philosophy seminar room, reading its copy of the work we call *Logical Investigations* in its original German, *Logische Untersuchungen*. She became convinced that Husserl was "*the* philosopher of our age." (Stein 1986: 219) When a cousin at the University of Göttingen invited Edith and her sister Erna to study there, Edith immediately told her family she would be going in the spring to study with Husserl. She had heard a former student of his say, "In Göttingen that's all you do: philosophize, day and night, at meals, in the street, everywhere. All you talk about is 'phenomena' [appearances]." (Stein 1986: 218) When New Year's Eve came, several of her friends celebrated by composing verses, and to Edith they sang:

Many a maiden dreams of "busserl" [kisses]
Edith, though, of naught but Husserl.
In Göttingen she soon will see
Husserl as real as real can be.

(Stein 1986: 220)

That spring Edith Stein was twenty-one years old and she "looked forward full of expectation to all that lay ahead." (Stein 1986: 239) Husserl had just turned fifty-five, on April 8, and perhaps he was looking backward, full of memories of all that lay behind. His elegance and dignity kept her from being overwhelmed. It was his head that she found handsome and impressive. His accent was Moravian—he had been born in Prossnitz, then part of the Austro-Hungarian Empire, now Prostéjov, about 135 miles east of Prague, Czechoslovakia, and 100 miles north of Vienna, Austria. He had discovered his passion for philosophy in Vienna, listening to the lectures of Franz Brentano. The "serene amiability" of the old city was still evident in him.

Even after twenty years, Stein remembered their first conversation. In the philosophy seminar room at the University of Göttingen, she was one of the newcomers who were presenting themselves to Husserl for acceptance as students. After the general discussion, he called the students to come up to him one by one. When she mentioned her name, he said:

"Dr. Reinach has spoken to me about you. How much of my work have you read?"
"The *Logische Untersuchungen.*"
"All of *Logische Untersuchungen*?" he asked me.
"Volume Two—all of it."
"All of Volume Two? Why, that's a heroic achievement!" he said, smiling. With that, I was accepted.

(Stein 1986: 249–50)

When Edith Stein saw Edmund Husserl face to face for the first time, "as real as real can be," what meaning was present in the fringe of awareness surrounding his brief physical appearance to her? Did she have a sense of her father, who had died suddenly before she had reached the age of two, as a kind and wise old man who would help her extraordinary intelligence and generous spirit unfold? Was this professor going to be a taskmaster who would inspire her to give herself fully to the mental exertion she was so well suited for? Did she feel in her attraction to Husserl an inexorable pull, the divine urgency of an ideal drawing her towards great passions and deeds? No doubt her face was flushed during their short talk—as it would be flushed, years later, when she was beginning to write her doctoral dissertation under Husserl's direction and was finding: "The writing would bring a rosy glow to my face, and an unfamiliar feeling of happiness surged through me." (Stein 1986: 377)

For his part, Husserl must have felt her admiration and excitement like a swallow of good brandy on a cold day. She was a vibrant young woman who had understood the book that had taken him many years to write. A woman philosopher was a rarity, and she, moreover, loved what had engaged him for so long. Like other students who had formed the Göttingen Philosophical Society, she was discovering the importance of his work. But recognition had been slow in arriving. Stein's interest in him leads me to think about accounts of his past.

As a postdoctoral student in 1883, Husserl had been profoundly affected in Vienna by Franz Brentano, who spoke of the mind primarily as "intentional," as tending toward meaning and as fulfilled by the significance of things present to it. He was moved as well by the writings of George Berkeley (1685–1753), Bishop of Cloyne in Ireland, who directly examined sense perception and saw mental life as an immediately felt, self-apparent activity. As his philosophical passion grew, Husserl made no attempt to study intentional acts of consciousness, particularly acts of sense perception, as though they were reducible to objects of natural science. For he found that intentional acts, like numbers, could be examined directly as they are lived and given in experience, as "things themselves," irreducible to natural spatio-temporal things.

In this way, Husserl's work avoids an assumption that many people make today: that ultimately molecules, genes, and cells, by biochemical and neurological processes, produce our emotional states, images, thoughts, even concepts of purpose or of spirit, which are thus only "metaphysical constructs." It is directly evident to me that I am perceiving this printed word now. It is by no means directly evident that my perceiving is caused by non-perceptual things I cannot perceive. Rather, it is a great act of faith to believe that tiny particles of matter are causing intentional activity. We well can wonder how spatially moving material things, even very tiny ones, might be able to "produce" the concept of 3 or the Idea of Equal, neither of which is a spatially moving material thing.

I have asked mathematicians, one from Russia, another from Italy, yet another from the USA, about the existence of the number 3, and they all acknowledged without hesitation that there is only one number 3. To Husserl, it was also quite obvious that there is only one of each number, even as we may name a number in a variety of ways. He writes:

> The Pythagorean theorem in the realm of propositions is one single proposition whenever I or anyone thinks it and proves it; just as the number four is one single number, whenever and by whomsoever it is thought or becomes consciously given by counting.
>
> (Husserl 1977b: 15)

Given that there is only one of each number, how can many varied molecules or neurons "cause" such a unique unchanging existence? Moreover, Plato and Socrates affirmed that "the Equal" is an actuality of its own kind and is not caused by material things. Rather, "the Equal" is itself the cause of whatever equality there is in materially appearing things. Sums may be equal, but not without the actuality of the Equal itself. Mathematicians spend a lot of time looking at numbers in relation to the Equal. Approximately fifteen minutes of honest talk with a pure mathematician is enough to show a neuroscience student that there is serious doubt that brain is the origin of mind, especially when the mind is counting, forming equations, or proving the Pythagorean theorem.

In any case, in order to notice our intentional activity, particularly our sense perception, as we are living it, we do not need to assume it is reducible to biochemical or neurological processes. More than a hundred years ago, Husserl avoided a growing prejudice of his century, mostly because he was keenly interested in watching the moments of consciousness themselves.

After completing *On the Concept of Number* (1887) at the age of twenty-eight and *Philosophy of Arithmetic* (1891) at thirty-two, Husserl spent most of the following decade preparing the *Logical Investigations*, a study of living intentionality and its meant objects. The labor was long, its external rewards few. In 1887, the year he married Malvine Steinschneider, his work on number at least allowed him to achieve "habilitation" at the University of Halle—permission to teach there as "privatdocent," as private teacher or lecturer recognized by the university but not paid by it. From 1887–1901, the year after the *Logical Investigations* were first published, he lived on fees provided by his students. Thus, for the first fourteen years of his marriage, he supported his family without having an official faculty position. When he moved in 1901 to the University of Göttingen, where Jacob and Wilhelm Grimm, the fairy tale compilers, had been professors in the 1830s, his situation improved only slightly. He was summoned there to a position created for him, as "extraordinary" or nontenured professor. His relation to his colleagues was difficult. His appointment

> had resulted from the decision of the minister of education against the will of the faculty. The representatives of the humanities faculty had predominantly philological and historical interests and had little appreciation for philosophy, whereas the natural scientists were disappointed that ... Husserl did not go over to the new faculty of natural sciences.
>
> (Landgrebe 1980: 69)

When he met Edith Stein in 1913, he had nevertheless begun to have a following. Around 1905 Husserl started to attract a number of students, at first mainly from Munich, "who developed a kind of group spirit and initiative which led gradually to the formation of the Göttingen Circle." (Spiegelberg 1965: 168) The originality of *Logical Investigations* surprised and heartened people, because it affirmed the importance of subjective mental life as something that can be studied directly, as itself. It considered "objectivity" in the widest possible sense of the term, as including not only natural spatial objects, but also lived nonspatial acts, as objects of our reflective attention.

Crucially, in the first paragraph of the Introduction to "Investigation III," Husserl distinguishes between non-independent parts and relatively independent parts of a whole. (Husserl 1970c: 435) For he is noticing that acts of awareness, and whatever they hold, are not concrete independent objects. Rather, awareness occurs in moments or phases that cannot exist without each other. These phases are not concrete, relatively independent objects, like this African violet plant and the table under it, for example. Rather, they are non-independent parts, phases, aspects, or moments that are inseparable from one another yet are well worth distinguishing as present now, or as past, or as about to be. Such inseparable yet distinct parts are like two sides of a coin: one side cannot exist without the other side, and so the two are said to be "reciprocally non-independent" of each other. When we examine moments of intentional activity and phases of appearance, as objects of our sustained attention, and when we notice that they are non-independent parts of a non-concrete whole, then we are students of phenomena or "phenomenologists," like the students Husserl attracted when he was in Göttingen.

Remarkably, at the end of the first chapter of the third logical investigation, Husserl refers to the "stream of consciousness" as having an essential order or "law of essence" that is an instance of a non-independence of parts: "the law, namely, that each actual, fulfilled conscious-present necessarily and continuously passes over into one that *has* just existed, so that our present conscious state makes continuous demands on our conscious future." (Husserl 1970c: 461) The distinct moments, phases, or parts of awareness, as present, past, or future, are non-independent of one another. Their interdependence is an abiding temporal form, an essential order, a continuous necessity, a mutual dependence which enables each part to be what is it.

If logical form is a necessary relation or order of statements, phenomenological form is a necessary relation or order of phenomena. A formal temporal order makes up the flux of awareness itself. Husserl speaks of time as "the immanent temporality which belongs to the phenomenological stream of consciousness itself." (Husserl 1970c: 461) As logical form is a non-independence of statements, so phenomenological form is a non-independence of phenomena as parts, phases, or moments that are present, past, and future.

For the next twenty years, Husserl studied and wrote about the temporal non-independence of appearing phases and intentional acts constituting awareness as a whole that is not concrete, like a plant or a table. Eventually the evidence of the inseparability of intentional awareness, phases of phenomena, and appearing concrete objects hit him so hard that he experienced a radical transformation of attitude, which he spoke of as a "breakthrough of this universal a priori of correlation between experienced object and manners of givenness"; this breakthrough, he said, "occurred during work on my *Logical Investigations*" and it "affected me so deeply that my whole subsequent life-work has been dominated by the task of systematically elaborating on this a priori of correlation." (Husserl 1970a: 166n) The correlation is the relation of reciprocal non-independence between an experienced object and its ways of being given to awareness in phases of appearance; it is a necessary relation between concrete objects and the flow of awareness which is not a concrete object. The correlation means that object and subject are non-independent, insofar as both are necessarily given to awareness in modes of appearance or phenomena. It is ironic, if not tragic, that Husserl hid in a footnote his declaration of an insight so central that it affected him most deeply and dominated his life-work.

In 1903, the first philosophy student to come to Göttingen from Munich rode his bicycle over 250 miles, and discussed *Logical Investigations* with Husserl from 3:00 p.m. to 3:00 a.m. Johannes Daubert found the work to be "a philosophical tonic bath." (Spiegelberg 1965: 171) He was joined later by several dozen others over the years, including Adolf Reinach, Moritz Geiger, Theodor Conrad, Dietrich von Hildebrand, Hedwig Conrad-Martius, Alexander Koyré, Jean Hering, Roman Ingarden, Fritz Kaufmann, Max Scheler, and Edith Stein. (Spiegelberg 1965: 169–70)

Husserl's new work, *Ideas toward a Pure Phenomenology* [the study of appearances] *and Phenomenological Psychology*, appeared in print in 1913, just in time for Stein's first seminar with him. His thought was available in a new way. He also made it a point to be at home one afternoon a week for students to discuss their questions and concerns with him. Stein was the first guest to arrive on the first "at home." She writes:

> Husserl had a home of his own on *Hohen Weg*, also at the edge of town where the road leads up to Rohns.... The house was built to his wife's specifications to provide for the family's needs. The Master's study was upstairs; it had a small balcony where he went to "meditate." The most important piece of furniture was an old leather sofa. He had gotten it in Halle after he received a grant while lecturing there. Usually, I had to sit at one end of the sofa. Even later, in Freiburg, we carried on our discussions on idealism back and forth from one end of that sofa to the other.
>
> (Stein 1986: 250–1)

Malvine, Husserl's wife, specified how the house was ordered. While her husband led a contemplative life, she was busy and practical. Women at that time rarely held jobs outside the home, and so she and the children were dependent on her husband's modest income. She considered it the "misfortune of her life" that Husserl had to

> live in Halle for twelve years [actually it was fourteen, from 1887 to 1901] as a privatdocent before he got a professorship. And even then, what he received was not a full professorship in Göttingen, but, instead, a special position created for him by the far-seeing and energetic but rather authoritarian Minister of Culture Althoff. Husserl's position on the faculty was a most embarrassing one.
>
> (Stein 1986: 251)

In a letter to Franz Brentano on January 1, 1905, Husserl had written:

> Certainly I have not been an ambitious *Privatdozent* eagerly looking out for
> the public and for the government. Such a one will publish both much and
> frequently. He will let himself be influenced in his problems and methods
> by the fashion of the day … and take special heed not to contradict them
> [the influential and famous ones] radically. I have done the exact opposite
> of all this, and hence it is not astonishing that for fully 14 years I have
> remained "*Privatdozent*" and have come even here (to Göttingen) only as
> "*Extraordinarius*" and against the wish of the faculty. For nine years I have
> published practically nothing, and I have made enemies of almost all the influ-
> ential people…. I have chosen my problems myself and have gone my own
> ways … I have acted this way not in order to be virtuous, but from a compelling
> necessity. The things themselves gained such power over me that I could not
> do otherwise – in spite of the burning desire for a modest position which could
> give me outward independence and the chance of a wider personal influence.
> Those were hard times for myself and for my family, and remembering what I
> had to bear, I do not like to be lumped with those climbers who have never lived
> for causes (die *Sachen* [the things themselves]), let alone suffered for them . …
>
> (Spiegelberg 1965: 89–90)

As Edith Stein remembers, the students called Husserl "the Master," a title he did
not like at all, and called his wife "Malvine." She was short, thin, "her gleaming-
black hair was smoothly parted; her brown eyes looked at the world with lively
interest, with curiosity, and always, with some degree of surprise." (Stein 1986:
251) Edith found her voice sharp, hard, and aggressive, but softened by a trace
of kindly humor. She was not kind to people she did not like, though she had
outspoken sympathies for the ones she did like. To Edith she was always sincerely
friendly, even before Edith became Husserl's assistant and rendered him valuable
service. Stein writes:

> When I was with her husband, she used to pop in midway through my visit to
> say she wanted to say hello. (The best discussions were suddenly interrupted
> in this manner.) She regularly attended Husserl's lectures and admitted to me
> later (though we had long been aware of it) that she made a habit of counting
> the students. She had no inner bond with philosophy.
>
> (Stein 1986: 251)

Malvine was determined to keep her three children away from philosophy.
Elisabeth, the oldest, was Edith's age and studied art history. Though like her
mother in looks, she had a softer and tenderer manner. Gerhart became a lawyer
but did not allow himself to be deprived of philosophy in later life. Wolfgang, the
youngest, had a great linguistic talent and was his mother's favorite. He was to
die in Flanders as a seventeen-year-old volunteer in the war. (Stein 1986: 251–2)

In graduate school I heard a rumor: Husserl had been surprised to learn that brothels still existed in Berlin. He was as modest and proper as he was innocent in such sexual matters. If he had not been, and if Edith Stein had not been similarly disposed, one of them might have become seductive. But there is no evidence at all that either one of them ever did. For Husserl, passion was bound with spiritual objects, and, besides, Malvine loved him.

The great passion when Edith Stein met Edmund Husserl was philosophical. She had left home to go study with him. At that time it was remarkable for a young woman, driven by philosophy, to leave her mother and live semi-independently in order to be involved in affairs of men. Few if any women then worked in business, government, university, or medicine, as many do today. A strong force impelled Stein—a desire for knowledge, an amazement at the power of thinking. I am interested in this force. During the last five decades, I have observed experiences that girls and women have had in beginning to reflect philosophically and think analytically. In these experiences, *logos*, the power of a word to express meaning, is bound up with strong passion, bodily energy, and compelling demand. A little girl just inside from playing outdoors washes her hands and stops to arrange the hand towel neatly on its rack. What is it in this girl, who has been playing outside in the dirt, that insists on order and beauty? A young woman discovers philosophy and her life is changed, whether or not she enters a convent. Her intellectual life is no ivory tower escape but is rather a full engagement of mind, body, and feeling. What moves her so radically?

The love of wisdom, *philo-sophia*, may draw a woman with a compelling necessity like the one Husserl experienced and wrote of in a letter to Franz Brentano: "I have acted this way not in order to be virtuous, but from a compelling necessity," as quoted just above. (Spiegelberg 1965: 89–90) But in many women, the response is whole, as women do not so easily overlook their bodies and feelings as men do. A male colleague who read the paragraphs above about Stein meeting Husserl says the writing makes him cringe with embarrassment. He did not expect to find emotional, bodily experience in philosophy. But for philosophical women such experience has often proved strong since girlhood. It moved Edith Stein to leave her mother, go study with Husserl, and follow *logos*. She never married and later became a contemplative Carmelite nun. She devoted herself fully to the life of soul as a way of knowing and loving not only the world she lived in, but also the God she found.

# Chapter 5

# Seeing the world as Husserl did

Husserl's work attracted Edith Stein and other members of the Göttingen Circle. He was not a professional academic philosopher whose thorough knowledge of traditional Western philosophy glowed in the dark. He was, rather, a mathematician pressed by "the things themselves"—the number continuum, the stream of consciousness, and the acts of intentional life. He was devoted to studying these nonmaterial "things" the way some people are devoted to their children or to a religious practice. His zeal was most evident in his continual writing: over forty thousand pages of it remain to this day. Daily he reflected and tried to see ever more clearly.

Husserl focused on intentional activity as it was happening. He did not compose logical arguments so much as spend time observing the intentional acts that are involved in any logical arguing. He distinguished aspects necessary to a whole as a way of describing the essence of that whole. For example, he looked at the world as a whole, and the necessary aspect that caught his interest was the fact that the world is looked at, and can be looked at, in many different ways. He saw that this fact of looking is essential: it is necessary to the world that it be noticed, lived in, and given, in a variety of different ways, whatever any specific way may be. And so it was the necessary interdependence of the aspects "outlook" and "world," not the many different outlooks themselves, which drew Husserl's attention. He sought to see the necessary parts that make up a whole. He referred to such seeking as a distinguishing of the essence of the whole.

Husserl recognized that outlook, as perspective or manner of being given to awareness, and world are inseparable. Distinguishing and describing a "basic outlook," he states in a passage from *Ideas*:

> Our first outlook upon life is that of natural human beings, imagining, judging, feeling, willing, *"from the natural standpoint."* Let us make clear to ourselves what this means in the form of simple meditations which we can best carry on in the first person.
>
> (Husserl 1958: 101, emphasis in original)

Husserl then describes how he is aware of a world, "spread out in space endlessly, and in time becoming and become, without end. I am aware of it, that means, first of all, I discover it immediately, intuitively, I experience it." (Husserl 1958: 101) Through sense perception things are "*for me simply there* ... whether or not I pay them special attention by busying myself with them, considering, thinking, feeling, willing." (Husserl 1958: 101, emphasis in original) It is not necessary that an object be present "precisely in my *field of perception*," as there are also objects "in my immediate co-perceived surroundings," and yet others reaching into "the limitless beyond," both spatially and temporally. (Husserl 1958: 101–2, emphasis in original) He concludes:

> In this way, when consciously awake, I find myself at all times, and without my ever being able to change this, set in relation to a world which, through its constant changes, remains one and ever the same. It is continually "present" for me, and I myself am a member of it. Therefore this world is not there for me as a mere *world of facts and affairs*, but, with the same immediacy, as a *world of values,* a *world of goods*, a *practical world.*
>
> (Husserl 1958: 103, emphasis in original)

Husserl describes this as evident: I am set in relation to a world continually present for me in a variety of ways, and I belong to it as a member. This state of affairs is a necessary aspect of intentional activity, the tending-toward meaning of awareness. It is important to note that intentional activity is not identical to the world. Husserl writes in another place: "Sensed red is red only in an equivocal sense, for red is the name of a real quality." (Husserl 1964: 25) Red belongs to a real concrete thing. But my intentional sense perception of the red thing is not a red thing; intentional receptivity and activity itself is colorless, immaterial, and nonspatial. Outlooks on the world are not identical to the spatio-temporal world that is lived in and looked at, even as outlook and world are inseparable.

The situation is remarkable: appearances, whatever they are, are inseparable from the world they make present, the world we live in as members. At the same time, appearances belong to experiencing subjectivity in intentional ways, as a flow of meaningfully lived experiencing—in the widest sense of the word "meaning." Appearances, world, and subjectivity are thus necessarily interrelated and interdependent, but they remain quite distinct. World and subject are distinct, even though appearances are inseparable from both, as appearances are the many varied ways in which the world is given to awareness as present. No wonder a student of Husserl's reported with amazement: "In Göttingen that's all you do: philosophize, day and night, at meals, in the street, everywhere. All you talk about is 'phenomena' [appearances]." (Stein 1986: 218)

# Chapter 6

# World without soul

Can the world exist without the soul or awareness? Scientists have assumed that it does. The modern age was built on a belief that it could. During twentieth-century wartime, many felt that the world was indeed barren of meaning. One of the most vivid sketches of such a feeling was made in words by Albert Camus, winner of the Nobel Prize for Literature in 1957.

Camus was killed in a car accident on January 4, 1960. His handwritten memoir of his childhood and youth in Algiers was found in the car wreckage. At the time of his death, he was still working on the manuscript. His wife Francine made the first typescript of the 144 unrevised pages. In 1994, thirty-four years after the accident, his daughter Catherine and her brother published the work as *Le premier homme* for Gallimard. In the editor's note to the subsequent English translation by David Hapgood, Catherine Camus writes:

> it is obvious that my father would never have published this manuscript as it is, first for the simple reason that he had not completed it, but also because he was a very reserved man and would no doubt have masked his own feelings far more in its final version. But ... it seems to me that one can most clearly hear my father's voice in this text because of its very rawness.
>
> (Camus 1995: vii)

In the manuscript we hear Camus at nightfall, gripped with dread:

> An enormous oblivion spread over them, and actually that was what this land gave out, what fell from the sky with the night over the three men returning to the village, their hearts made anxious by the approach of night, filled with that dread that seizes all men in Africa when the sudden evening descends on the sea, on the rough mountains and the high plateaus ... his father ... too was returned to that immense oblivion that was the ultimate homeland of the men of his people, the final destination of a life that began without roots ...
>
> (Camus 1995: 193–4)

Enormous oblivion of night, dark sky over dark land—this finally is the world. Life began without roots, and the ultimate homeland of the men of his people is immense oblivion, bleak and raw. We are like foundlings, "found and lost children who built transient towns in order to die forever in themselves and in others." (Camus 1995: 194)

Yet, as I read and write outdoors, two small birds with long beaks and gold chests hop briefly onto the fence, look at me, and chirp. The huge trees above us have not lost their minds but are dropping leaves and acorns in preparation for a cold season ahead. Holding future life, far from dumb, seeds in purple pods hang from the vine on the fence and quietly absorb the sun's warmth. I continue to read Camus: "As if the history of men ... [were] evaporating under the constant sun with the memory of those who made it ..." (Camus 1995: 194) Again Camus finds memory to be an immense oblivion.

Does our lived time, our suffering, the smell of skin, finally evaporate under a sun that itself never ceases to burn? Do earth and sky remain as an empty place, into which life comes and goes? The world existing in and by itself—is that what exists ultimately? I wonder, as Camus continues: "Now the night was rising from the land itself and began to engulf everything, the dead and the living, under the marvelous and ever-present sky." (Camus 1995: 194) Monsieur Camus, why do you say there is no past and our lives are destroyed after we live them? As I strain in questioning, Camus goes on in acute misery:

> No, he would never know his father, who would continue to sleep over there, his face forever lost in the ashes. There was a mystery about that man, a mystery he had wanted to penetrate. But after all there was only the mystery of poverty that creates beings without names and without a past, that sends them into the vast throng of the nameless dead who made the world while they themselves were destroyed forever.
>
> (Camus 1995: 194)

Camus's father had died in World War I and had left the child without roots, tradition, or history. His mother was nearly deaf and rarely showed affection. He lived in poverty with her, his brother, his grandmother, and his uncle, under the grandmother's crude whip, in a small four-room apartment in Algiers. Through the action of Louis Germain, his teacher, he attended the *lycée*, and the world opened up for him. Yet he still felt, at least sometimes, that the world was ultimately a bare horizon of earth and sky, belonging to no one—an enduring emptiness that held no personal names as it overcame everyone. Existence as individual suffocation, a gas chamber and crematorium: while I ponder this, another bird flies to me, shakes his head, and leaves promptly. I pick up the pages of Camus again:

> For it was just that that his father had in common with the men ... : the silence of anonymity; it enveloped blood and courage and work and instinct .... And he ... wandering through the night of the years in the land of oblivion where

each one is the first man, where he had to bring himself up, without a father, having never known those moments when a father would call his son, after waiting for him to reach the age of listening, to tell him the family's secret, or a sorrow of long ago, or the experience of his life ... like all the men born in this country who, one by one, try to learn to live without roots and without faith, and today all of them are threatened with eternal anonymity ...

(Camus 1995: 194–5)

In the manuscript, Camus slips briefly into the first person and says: "The Mediterranean separates two worlds in me, one where memories and names are preserved in measured spaces, the other where the wind and sand erase all trace of men on the open ranges." (Camus 1995: 196) Then he continues in the third person:

He had tried to escape from anonymity, from a life that was poor, ignorant, and mulish; he could not live that life of blind patience, without words, with no thought beyond the present. He had traveled far and wide, had built, had created, had loved people and abandoned them, his days had been full to overflowing. And yet now ... he thought of the worn and green-encrusted gravestones he had just left, acknowledging with a strange sort of pleasure that death would return him to his true homeland and, with its immense oblivion, would obliterate the memory of that alien and ordinary man who had grown up, had built in poverty, without help or deliverance, on a fortunate shore and in the light of the first mornings of the world, and then alone, without memories and without faith, had entered the world of the men of his time and its dreadful and exalted history.

(Camus 1995: 196–7)

His father had died young and his mother could barely hear. Camus had little sense of the continuum of life: he was "the first man." I know of no evidence that he gazed at numbers or wondered at their infinite series of infinite series. Instead, there is abundant evidence that he loved colors, sounds, textures of the present moment. After thirty years, he still remembered the taste and smell of a fried potato crumb, savored at the beach with his friends. (Camus 1995: 50) He was interested in experiencing real things, not in making philosophical distinctions: I never heard him suggest that consciousness and world are distinct yet interdependent. Near death he anticipated the obliteration of all he was and had struggled to become. He felt the world of wind and sand covering all trace of men—no one, nothing remembering even our names.

Husserl was not a philosophical father to Camus as he had been to Edith Stein or was to me. He did not call to Camus as son, "after waiting for him to reach the age of listening," as Camus had imagined a father doing, and did not say simply and directly: "Consciousness and memory are nonmaterial and are irreducible to physical processes. Something appearing is impossible without some degree of awareness it is appearing to." Had Husserl's writing been accessible and made understandable to a wide audience, it might have shown a sense of continuum to the younger man who felt he was the first man. Indeed, Husserl had wanted to pass his work on. Yet beyond a circle of academics, his accomplishment was little known. Only in his last few years did he begin to enter the public world speaking in a loud voice—after he had already been silenced in Germany. He was neglected by the academic successor he had named, he died, and the philosophizing he had wanted to give over as an inheritance was not acknowledged as widely as it deserves to be. Camus ended his life with a view of the world apparently quite different from Husserl's.

Camus suffered what many men of the twentieth century did. He felt he was without roots and faith, and the world was the enduring sky and land—immediate material reality into which conscious life was somehow appearing and disappearing. Right before him, natural objectivity seemed to be swallowing up people, culture, ideals. Similar to those who believed in natural science as a metaphysical world-view, Camus uncritically assumed that consciousness comes from purely material, natural, objective reality, and that it is nothing of itself, in its own character. So, despite his success in the world of men, Camus lived in philosophical poverty, at least according to the manuscript he left behind. He did not live with a sense of number or the Equal as genuinely existing. He had not witnessed the distinction of consciousness from world. He did not seem to be aware of appearances as both subjective and objective. No one had shown him how to look at these things, never mind why they might be worthy of sustained attention.

Earth and sky, sand and wind, contain life anonymously and then bury it all: the world appeared to Camus in this way. But in this experience as recorded, he did not notice the appearing and his own outlook as necessary aspects of the world. Even less did he notice any "ring" of indeterminate appearing related to more determinate, focused appearing—or if he did, he did not describe it as a way of appearing. For he lived in the real things he directly viewed before him, in the sense of the Greek word *theōrein*, "to view," but he did not notice his own viewing. He was "entirely absorbed in considering the object," as Edith Stein would have said about him, in terms of what she wrote:

> It is possible to conceive of a subject only living in theoretical [viewing] acts having an object world facing it without ever becoming aware of itself and its consciousness, without "being there" for itself. But this is no longer possible as soon as this subject not only perceives, thinks, etc., but also feels. For as it feels it not only experiences objects, but it itself. It experiences emotions as coming from the "depth of its 'I'."
>
> (Stein 1989: 98)

Stein wrote these words as part of her doctoral dissertation, composed under Husserl's direction and filling a gap in his philosophy. In her work, she was describing empathy as an intentional activity of its own kind, one she practiced readily. She knew that it is through feeling that a subject experiences and recognizes itself, insofar as emotions come from a depth of subjectivity. Had she been able to read *The First Man*, she would immediately have noticed its absorption in directly considering material objects rather than personal emotions. Yet, like many readers of Camus, she would have been aware of the feeling expressed indirectly though forcefully throughout the book: loneliness, dread, misery, sadness, despair. Through empathy, she would know his feeling as nonetheless the feeling of someone other. She would heartily affirm it as truly existing, for she recognized that subjectivity exists just as much as material objectivity does, and just as much as Ideas do. She had a philosophical spirit that helped her affirm a wide sense of existence.

# Chapter 7

# Husserl, Jung, and the "unconscious"

Husserl brought a focus to the stream of experience that enabled him to notice as present not only directly perceived things, but also intentional activities through which these things are present. Moreover, he noticed that the intentional activities have indirectly perceived or "co-present" aspects. He described a "*co-present* margin" or "continuous ring around the actual field of perception," and he wrote that what is actually perceived, as well as "what is more or less clearly co-present and determinate (to some extent at least), is partly pervaded, partly girt about with a *dimly apprehended depth or fringe of indeterminate reality*." (Husserl 1958: 102, emphasis in original) In this way, as "depth" and "fringe," Husserl spoke about what Jung called "the unconscious," although Husserl would not have thought to use the term "unconscious" since it was a depth or fringe of consciousness itself that he was noticing. Husserl realized that, if he could speak of a phenomenon at all, it had to be at least partially apparent, noticed, or "apprehended" in awareness. For Jung, however, it was easier to speak of such indirectly noticed phenomena simply as "unconscious," since they are so dimly known.

Husserl recognized that the world is present not as a concrete whole, not as a thing within his grasp or anyone else's, and not even as a well-defined objectivity. Only a very small part of the world is actually here now. The rest of the world is indeterminately given. When Husserl says the "misty horizon that can never be completely outlined remains necessarily there," he is not referring directly to the anonymous, concrete earth and sky Camus writes about in *The First Man*. (Husserl 1958: 102) Rather, Husserl is referring to the living horizon of unfocused consciousness that accompanies each moment of focused perception. This horizon or "continuous ring around the actual field of perception" indicates the rather vague limit and relation of the unfocused to the focused. Perception of something right there is inseparable from memories, hopes, images, feelings, and other significance as given simultaneously by the corresponding intentional activities of remembering, expecting, imagining, and feeling. Direct sense perception depends on them all. A complex meaningful activity pervades and supports perception in mostly unnoticed ways that have thus been called "unconscious" or "subconscious." We are aware of much of the world indirectly and vaguely, though we might not think so. Even Camus was aware of much that he did not acknowledge explicitly.

I have asked students in a philosophy class to hold their arms up and slowly move them away towards their sides. At a certain point, their arms are visible only peripherally, and then they are not visible at all, although they can be felt. Our field of actual vision, strictly speaking, is quite small. The little bit we are seeing is still the world, inasmuch as the world is a continuum not only extending beyond the here and now, but also depending on the here and now. Strictly speaking, we have only a little bit of the world at a time, a limited focus of perception; but that limited bit cannot be present without much that is meant in unfocused, indeterminate ways, as depth or fringe of consciousness.

The Latin word *focus* means "hearth, fire-place; pyre, altar; (*fig.*) home." (Kidd 1961: 138) A focus of perception with a ring of indeterminate awareness is a hearth, a fireplace to live by, and a home. A focus of perception that aims to exclude the unfocused, however, is a burning altar or pyre of sacrifice that would burn up what surrounds and pervades it: the margin of dim consciousness in which the rest of the world and the rest of time are present indirectly. Without some notice of this "zone of indeterminacy" that Husserl says is infinite, there is no sense of history or roots—just oblivion in which each one is "the first man." While an overly focused perception may attempt to burn up any acknowledgement of something besides itself, nevertheless, the "misty horizon that can never be completely outlined remains necessarily there." (Husserl 1958: 102) This enduring living horizon belongs to subjective experiencing, not to spatial objects considered as though they might be able to exist independently of perception and its indeterminate "fringe." Yet the famous twentieth-century logician and philosopher Bertrand Russell for most of his life sought to clear away the indeterminate; he said, "I like precision. I like sharp outlines. I hate misty vagueness." (Russell 1961: 30) The great psychologist William James, however, born in New York in 1842, well appreciated both the clear and the not so clear.

Husserl's use of the term "fringe" can be traced to William James, whom Husserl discovered through his friend, Carl Stumpf, who had met James in Prague in 1882. Twelve years later, in an article of 1894, Husserl referred to James's "stream of thought" and "fringes." James's *Principles of Psychology*, particularly chapter XII, had affected Husserl's developing sense of "intentionality" as a creative achievement and as occurring in various modes. (Spiegelberg 1965: 113–16) Husserl wrote about James's *Psychology* in his diary of 1906:

> I saw how a daring and original man did not let himself be held down by tradition and attempted to really put down what he saw and to describe it. Probably this influence was not without significance for me, although I could read and understand precious few pages. Indeed, to describe and to be faithful, this was absolutely indispensable. To be sure, it was not until my article of 1894 that I read larger sections and took excerpts from them.
>
> (Spiegelberg 1965: 114)

Husserl had first heard about "intentionality," a term for the tending of consciousness toward meaning, in the Vienna lectures of Franz Brentano in 1883, and for decades afterward he corresponded with Brentano. Surprisingly, Sigmund Freud also had been a student of Brentano's.

There are other coincidences between Husserl and Freud. In 1856, Freud was born in Moravia, where Husserl was born in 1859. When Freud died in London in 1939, it was the year after Husserl's death. Except for his first four years and his last one, Freud "spent his entire life in Vienna." (Ellenberger 1970: 418) Edith Stein, upon meeting Husserl for the first time, noted that his "speech at once betrayed his Austrian birth: he came from Moravia and had studied in Vienna. His serene amiability also had something of old Vienna about it." (Stein 1986: 249) Freud's chief work, *The Interpretation of Dreams*, appeared in 1900, the same year Husserl's *Logical Investigations* was published.

Moreover, Freud had a creative illness which resulted in a deep transformation of personality that was "indissolubly united with the conviction of having discovered a grandiose truth that must be proclaimed to mankind." (Ellenberger 1970: 450) For Freud, the great truth he discovered was the psychoanalytic method and a new theory of the mind, which he proclaimed in *The Interpretation of Dreams*. In describing the creative illness and transformation Freud underwent in coming to his discovery, Ellenberger writes:

> It is as if the individual had followed the call of Saint Augustine, "Seek not abroad, turn back into thyself, for in the inner man dwells the truth." [Augustine's Latin is given in note 141.] "*Noli foras ire, in teipsum redi; in interiore homine habitat veritas.*" *De vera religione*, Chap. 39, par. 72.
>
> (Ellenberger 1970: 449–50, 555)

These same lines from Augustine appear in Latin in the main text, with an English translation in a footnote, at the very end of Husserl's *Cartesian Meditations: An Introduction to Phenomenology*, which he began working on in 1929, and delivered in Paris at the Sorbonne. Through studying consciousness immanently for a long time, Husserl discovered what has been called "the phenomenological method" and a new view of the mind, as a great truth which he proclaimed with a call to philosophical reflection: "Return into you yourself!"

The fact that Husserl ended a great work with a quotation from a classical Latin author—having taken the same lines that Ellenberger later uses in describing Freud—shows in a wide sense that Husserl was part of the same classically educated European culture that Freud was part of. Both had studied Latin, not for speaking, but rather for writing, and as "a method of acquiring an ever-increasing capacity for mental concentration and mental synthesis, which might also be compared with the study of mathematics." (Ellenberger 1970: 262) At the beginning of his chief work, Freud inserted a motto from Virgil's *Aeneid*, VII, v. 312: "*Flectere si nequeo Superos, Acheronta movebo!* (If Heaven I cannot bend, then Hell I will arouse!)" (Ellenberger 1970: 452) Freud revolutionized psychology, but not without letting the Furies out of Hell—this he announced in Latin elegance.

Perhaps the most remarkable of the coincidences involving Husserl and Freud, who apparently never met personally, is that Freud attended lectures of Franz Brentano in Vienna and was, like Husserl, greatly influenced by them. Brentano, a Dominican priest and professor of philosophy at Würzburg, left the Catholic Church because he could not accept the teaching of papal infallibility. In Vienna he had to start his career all over again as a "privatdocent." His new psychology was based on "intentionality," a concept he revived from medieval scholastic philosophy, and it drew the interest of distinguished ladies of Vienna, Franz Kafka, and Rudolf Steiner, among others.

Yet the only mention Freud makes of Brentano in his writings is a footnote reference in Freud's *Jokes and the Unconscious*; apparently, Brentano had made elaborate plays on words and had "imagined a new kind of riddle he called *dal-dal-dal* that became the rage in Viennese salons." (Ellenberger 1970: 541–2) Despite Freud's lack of explicit acknowledgement of Brentano's great influence on him, James Ralph Barclay at Idaho State College in 1961 carefully traced several of Freud's concepts specifically back to Brentano and found:

> The notion of intentionality appears in Freud in the modified form of a psychic energy channeled toward instinctual goals and wish-fulfillment. Brentano's "intentional existence" became Freud's "cathexis." To Freud, as to Brentano, perception was not a passive process but an activity endowed with psychic energy.
>
> (Ellenberger 1970: 542)

Similarly, for Husserl "intentionality" is a spontaneous tending toward meaning that characterizes consciousness of anything; it is a tending toward "fulfillment," the presence of the meant. The tending toward meaning occurs in different modes, such as perceiving, remembering, imagining, and expecting, insofar as each of these acts aims at something meant in a different way—as perceived, remembered, imagined, or expected. Each tending or aiming thus finds its specific fulfillment in the "intentional existence" of the thing meant, the actual presence of the thing (in the widest sense of the word "thing") as a phenomenon of awareness—as perceived existence, remembered existence, imagined existence, or expected existence. Thus, presence in memory, imagination, and expectation are as important as presence in sense perception. The real world includes not only objects of sense perception, but also objects of the past, potential ones, others hovering near as about to happen … all as existing *intentionally* and affecting us powerfully with their reality.

For both Freud and Husserl, it is clear that the world is much more than material, physical, spatial objects: the world also includes the genuine intentional existence of what is remembered, imagined, dreamed, and felt, as truly present, as demanding attention, and as necessarily related to subjectivity. The works of both Freud and Husserl cry out: "Return into you yourself!"

Both Freud and Husserl recognized that the "psychic energy" of intentional life, the being in the soul, is not under the deliberate direction of an individual, but rather flows in its own way as knowable to itself. While an individual has some degree of ability to direct attention this way or that, the stream of intending goes "as it will." Brentano's view of intentionality thus inspired Freud, as James Ralph Barclay shows, even as it inspired Husserl in strikingly similar ways.

Unlike Freud, Husserl did not call intentionality "libido" or "the unconscious," and he did not write specifically about dreams, hypnotic states, visions, psychoses, or psychoanalyses. Rather, he turned to psychology as a science and examined its basic concepts and presuppositions. At a time when experimental psychology was the rage, Husserl insisted that a phenomenological clarification come first in which intentional acts of consciousness are examined, distinguished, and described. Such clarification would allow psychologists to see that consciousness is not a spatio-temporal object, but is rather a focus of awareness which has depth and indeterminacy continually accompanying it.

Still, I feel that James, Brentano, Husserl, and Freud were living in a continuum of soul which was holding a sense of "intentionality" and its "fringe" that they all knew at least dimly and were trying to focus on and describe. While these men came near one another only briefly in the focused daylight of consciousness, their awareness was nevertheless interconnected, as quite close in the unfocused darkness. They were drawn by the same Idea, whatever it might be called, and they lived in service to it. As Socrates and Plato had recognized, an Idea is not a private possession.

# Part II

# Observing and understanding the flow of phenomena

# Chapter 8

# Transfinite whole

Husserl was a mathematician before he was a philosopher. His doctorate was in mathematics; he read philosophy mostly on his own after obtaining his advanced degree. As a mathematician and colleague of Georg Cantor at the University of Halle, Husserl well knew the concept of "transfinite number" as defined by Cantor. In *Husserliana XII*, Lothar Eley says that when the younger Husserl arrived at Halle in 1886, Cantor was already well established yet was to take a lively scientific and personal interest in Husserl. (Husserl 1970b: xxiii)

When the concept of "transfinite number" is present to focused attention, it is far from adequately present, and so it is at the same time a symbol or representation in the margins of awareness. It can be felt as a mighty force, like the one Husserl felt, as referred to earlier: "I have acted this way not in order to be virtuous, but from a compelling necessity." (Spiegelberg 1965: 89–90) He experienced an animating energy that was powerful enough to enable him to live in the world, inasmuch as philosophy was the mission of his life and he *had to* philosophize. (Husserl 1968: 161, emphasis in original) For Husserl, philosophizing meant paying utmost attention to spirit as existing here and now, as the life of consciousness. He had to attend to this study of consciousness every day or not live. Far from being merely an abstract thought, the concept of "transfinite number" both showed and symbolized the continuum that was beyond him, that he was nevertheless part of; the continuum compelled his attention and studying it made him "able to live in this world."

When Husserl noticed his awareness at a given moment, he was observing "something" that was not and is not a material thing, and he observed that it was not. The actions and passions of living experience—seeing, touching, remembering, thinking, feeling, for example—occur in time, but not as spatial objects. We too can notice them as we live them actively and passively. Husserl habitually turned his attention to his perception in the moment, whether it was the perception of a sound, or of the number continuum, or of his awareness of the sound and the number continuum. He observed his perception directly, as a complex yet mostly spontaneous accomplishment of awareness. He wrote over 40,000 pages describing what he found. He was dedicated to an infinite task.

Husserl did not reduce the mental life he was observing to physical processes or chemical activity he was not observing. He examined mental acts themselves, as interesting in their own right. In his earlier writings, he studied the steps we take in doing mathematics and logic. In later writing, he studied the sounding of a tone in time. Reading his descriptions of sense perception as a living, temporal event changed my attitude irrevocably. I had not noticed my perceiving before; I had not even known that I could. Husserl pointed to moments of silence; then to moments of a tone sounding as it was beginning, enduring, ending; then to silence again. I had previously just listened to the tone. Now, with Husserl, I was noticing moments of the tone sounding, as expected, as given, as past, as continually being related to one another. These were moments of consciousness. They still are moments of consciousness; they have not become something else. I remember them as having been lived and as moments of reflective perceiving.

Husserl showed me how to observe awareness by his repeated attempts to observe it himself. I could see right away that I did not need two different successive moments during which to notice, first, a sound and, then, my awareness of it. For, sound and awareness of the sound are simultaneous and inseparable, even as they are distinct, in each moment of hearing. Both sound and awareness are aspects of given objectivity, and now the word "object" comes to refer not only to concrete things, but also to aspects of perceiving—to the lived moments as phases of both appearing sound and perceiving awareness—for both sound and awareness are given as objective, as "objects" in the widest sense of the term, as anything to which attention may be directed. I used to notice just the sound; in studying Husserl, I noticed more of what was present together as a whole.

In 1968, I took my first course on Husserl at Duquesne University in Pittsburgh. I remember riding the bus to class, as my mind was boiling. Husserl's approach was simple, his insights elemental, and his language hard. My awareness was hit like a baseball and flew, but not out and far—rather, in and near, into the present instant. I never got tired of studying awareness as it was happening. I began to feel the compelling energy motivating his study as it drew my own interest more and more.

Years after I left Duquesne, some works by Edith Stein attracted my attention. Like Simone de Beauvoir, she had only been mentioned by my professors as a side note, as student, assistant, and colleague of a famous man philosopher. When, however, I opened her books and began reading, and whenever I did so long afterwards, I could not stop reading them for several hours, and they made me cry—for this brilliant engaging woman philosopher who had been murdered at Auschwitz in 1942.

Edith Stein was born Jewish, studied with Husserl, and one day, at the home of friends who had gone out, discovered a book (I think it was *Interior Castle*) by Teresa of Avila, a medieval Spanish Carmelite nun, reformer, and mystic. Stein stayed up all night reading Teresa, and in the morning decided to become a Carmelite, a contemplative nun. Years later, she did. Seldom visiting Husserl after completing her assistantship with him, she nonetheless had a strong philosophical and religious bond with him, which neither distance nor death destroyed. Stein was remarkable in having such bonds.

I learned from Stein's autobiography that she and her colleagues called Husserl "the Master," although he did not like the name. Through Stein I also came to see that Husserl, whom she recognized as "the" greatest philosopher of the twentieth century, was nonetheless a finite human being. He suffered loss, deception, degradation. His younger son, Wolfgang, died in Flanders during war. A Nazi took his place at the University. He was later silenced in Germany. Yet philosophy continued to be the mission of his life, even though he had not started out as a philosophy student.

Husserl was born on April 8, 1859. A passion for the infinite and the ideal led him as a young man to study astronomy at the University of Leipzig, and mathematics at the University of Berlin. He received his doctorate in 1882, at the age of twenty-three, after studying calculus under Karl Weierstrass. When he came to the University of Halle to teach, Georg Cantor became his close colleague and friend, as I mentioned earlier. These and other great mathematicians were at the time concerned with aggregates of infinite series. An aggregate is a sum, mass, or assemblage of particulars, a total amount, a whole. An "aggregate of an infinite series" seems to be a contradiction in terms, for "infinite" means "boundless, not finite, unlimited, innumerable." How, then, can an infinite series, which has no end of being counted, be aggregated into one sum, a total amount, a whole? How is an infinite series of infinite series, that is incomprehensible if not uncanny, aggregated in the essence of a unitary whole? These questions are a starting point for philosophical wonder.

Is it possible to have a definite concept, a sense of the essence, of an infinite series? After many years of inner struggle, Georg Cantor discovered that "infinite numbers" were possible; that is, he had a logically consistent concept of them, despite denials among philosophers and theologians that they could exist. In articles Cantor published in 1887 and 1888, and collected into a little book in 1890, he wrote:

> All so-called proofs of the impossibility of actually infinite numbers are, as may be shown in every particular case and also on general grounds, false in that they begin by attributing to the numbers in question all the properties of finite numbers, whereas the infinite numbers, if they are to be thinkable in any form, must constitute quite a new kind of number as opposed to the finite numbers, and the nature of this new kind of number is dependent on the nature of things and is an object of investigation, but not of our arbitrariness or our prejudice.
>
> (Cantor 1955: 73–4)

Infinite numbers exist; they are not finite numbers; they constitute a kind of number that is new to us. We do not create them arbitrarily or merely presuppose them. They exist objectively in a logically consistent concept.

To recognize the existence of infinite numbers, Cantor suggests that we first consider an aggregate of distinct things as itself one whole, as one general concept distinct from other general concepts. We must not look at the many things that are aggregated, but rather at the whole they make. Cantor writes: "Every aggregate of distinct things can be regarded as a unitary thing in which the things first mentioned are constitutive elements." (Cantor 1955: 74)

Consider, then, an aggregate; forget about what its elements are; then disregard the order of the elements. For example, consider the aggregate of all the positive even integers, 2, 4, 6, and so on, where 2 is the first element, 4 the second, and so on. Now disregard, as much as possible, the fact that the elements are positive and even. This may not be too difficult to do. After all, the aggregate of all the positive odd integers (1, 3, 5, and so on) is a lot like the aggregate of positive even integers, and both are like the aggregate of negative even integers (–2, –4, –6, and so on) and the aggregate of negative odd integers (–1, –3, –5, and so on).

Now disregard the order of elements in any of these aggregates, the position of each element in the series. Consider all the elements as still there, but without a specified order, or with any possible order. What remains is a general concept of an infinite series of elements, a "cardinal number," the amount of the whole. As Cantor says:

> If we abstract *both* from the nature of the elements and from the order in which they are given, we get the 'cardinal number' or 'power' of the aggregate, a general concept in which the elements, as so-called units, have so grown organically into one another to make a unitary whole that no one of them ranks above the others.
>
> (Cantor 1955: 74)

We have achieved a general concept, not by counting all the elements, but rather by abstracting from them as individuals and by grasping them altogether as a whole. That "unitary whole" is a "cardinal number."

The cardinal number of an aggregate is thus a general concept, without regard to the order of its given elements; the same concept, as including the order of the elements, is their "ordinal number" or "ordinal type." The cardinal number is not a count, not an enumeration, of all the elements in the aggregate, but rather a concept of them as a whole. The ordinal number is the concept of the cardinal number with the order of elements given and included in the concept. We can see this for ourselves rather clearly.

But if we continue, something surprising happens. Let us then continue slowly and carefully until it does. Let us call the aggregate of positive even integers "M," the aggregate of positive odd integers "N," the aggregate of negative even integers "P," and the aggregate of negative odd integers "Q." Let us see if any of these aggregates of infinite series is "equivalent" to any other. They are obviously not equal but may be "equivalent." "Equivalence of two series A, B" means that, for each element of A, there is a distinct element of B that can be paired with it, and for each element of B, there is a distinct element of A that can be paired with it. "Equivalence" here is a one-to-one correspondence between elements of the two series, A, B. "Equivalent" does not mean "equal."

Consider the aggregate of positive even integers "M" and the aggregate of positive odd integers "N." It is obvious that, for each element of M, there is a distinct element of N that can be paired with it, and, that for each element of N, there is a distinct element of M that can be paired with it. We will not run out of elements, in either aggregate, in the pairing. There is a one-to-one correspondence between elements of M and N. M and N are equivalent. By similar considerations, we see that M, N, P, and Q, are all equivalent to one another. They have the same cardinal number or general concept. By paying attention to M, N, P, and Q, we have a clearer sense of their cardinal number or general concept.

Here comes a surprise, perhaps like falling off a cliff. Now let "R" be the infinite series of finite numbers. Let "S" be the infinite series of numbers between 2 and 3. R and S are equivalent, because, for each element of R, there is an element of S, and for each element of S, there is an element of R. In pairing them, we do not run out of elements in either series. Thus, R and S are equivalent, and both have the same cardinal number. But S is a part of R. Therefore, a part is equivalent to what it is part of. In fact, it happens often that, with infinite aggregates, two aggregates are equivalent, they have the same cardinal number, and one is a part of the other. An abyss opens up, as we look farther and farther down into an infinite series of infinite series.

This glimpse of the infinite reminds me of the *Discourse on Metaphysics* (1686) of G. W. von Leibniz, who developed the calculus at the same time that Sir Isaac Newton did, though neither one knew of the other's work at the time. In the *Discourse*, Leibniz thinks of individual things as "substances" or subjects that "stand under" or are subject to their attributes, qualities, or predicates. The concept of "substance" had been a key concept in Western philosophy since the time of Aristotle, but John Locke in the seventeenth century wrote that it really did not mean anything as it cannot be perceived directly. Locke saw "substance" as imaginary, artificial, and vague. Scientists, mathematicians, and philosophers rarely use the term today.

In any case, while Leibniz and his calculus indeed helped modern science and mathematics develop, he himself could not abandon the ancient concept of "substance" when thinking philosophically. For he saw that any individual thing, call it "$S_0$," or "S sub-zero," does have attributes, qualities, or predicates, that can be predicated or said about it as subject. In fact, $S_0$ may have an infinite series of predicates, call them "$P_0$, $P_1$, $P_2$, and so on," as belonging to it, attributable to it, qualifying it, such that $S_0$ is $P_0$, $P_1$, $P_2$, and so on. The subject is the whole of all that can ever be truly said about it. Thus, the whole includes an infinite series of particular details about it that relate it—directly to some, indirectly to all other—individual subjects, call them $S_1$, $S_2$, $S_3$, and so on, in the universe. For Leibniz, a subject or substance is an individual, not a kind, type, or classification of individuals. Each substance is unique and has its own direct or indirect relation to every other substance in the universe. Each has its own individual essence—its own aggregate of predicates that tell what it is.

Accordingly, the concept or essence of an individual thing, which Leibniz still called a "substance" and understood as a subject of its predicates, is a whole which includes an infinite series of predicates, insofar as the substance bears some relation, whether direct or indirect, to every other substance in the universe. This inclusion of an infinite series is modern. The ancient Greeks abhorred the inclusion of an infinite series of predicates in expressing the essence or concept of a substance; they felt such a series had to end somewhere in order for its elements to exist really. An infinite series cannot be perceived or counted directly. The Greeks saw it as imaginary, artificial, and vague. For them, an individual thing and its definition must be fixed, determinate, limited, and brought to an end, in order to exist and be known.

Leibniz and his calculus, however, went beyond the finite series. He asserted that a concept of an actually existing individual substance is able to include an infinite series of predicates about that substance, "although God alone could recognize them all." (Leibniz 1962: 14) For, included in the definition of the essence of each thing is its relation to every other thing, whether in near relation or in far. If the universe is a whole, a continuum of substances, then each depends in some way on all the others in order to be what it is. Each has qualities that correspond to qualities in the others.

As we make more precise our awareness of an individual substance, we see that the universe as the original continuum "breaks up" into parts, the individuals, that are equivalent not only to one another, but also to the whole universe itself (as we noticed, S is a part of R; such a part is equivalent to what it is part of). For the individual substance, the part, "expresses, although confusedly, all that happens in the universe, past, present and future, deriving thus a certain resemblance to an infinite perception or power of knowing." (Leibniz 1962: 15) The parts that are equivalent to the whole are also equivalent to one another. "And since all other substances express this particular substance and accommodate themselves to it, we can say that it exerts its power upon all the others in imitation of the omnipotence of the creator." (Leibniz 1962: 15) The others exert their power on a given particular substance too, although Leibniz does not say so explicitly. He seems to be a bit carried away in talking about an infinite power of knowing and an imitation of the omnipotence of the creator.

Without getting carried away too far, we can pause now and review what we have just been doing. In a preliminary focus on the concept "transfinite number" as a concept of an unending series as a unitary whole, we have noticed with Leibniz that the universe as original continuum appears to be "separated" or "broken up into parts" insofar as the individuals are distinguished as parts equivalent in different ways to the whole. Like each counting number, each individual is a unique view of the whole insofar as the concept of each includes an infinite series of possible statements about the individual's relation to everything else. At the same time, when an individual becomes aware of possible self-knowledge with respect to the infinite series of relations to others, that particular one has a sense of the original continuum; this sense deepens the individual view and gives meaning to the individual life. Of course, the individual is not equal to the whole, but only equivalent. Nevertheless, there is not only a "breaking up" but also a "deepening" in recognizing the concept of the unending series as a whole.

Thus the mathematical becomes philosophical for us as we try to understand the concept "transfinite number" and find ourselves considering the universe as original continuum that breaks up into parts that are each infinitely deepened. This consequence of studying mathematics was not surprising to Leibniz, for whom mathematics and philosophy, not to mention, politics, theology, and other studies, expressed aspects of a whole. For Husserl, mathematics led to a study of the acts that are performed in doing mathematics and logic; some time after completing his doctorate and other works in mathematics, he wrote *Logical Investigations* in which he showed how statements about numbers and reasoning, even as lived subjectively, have evidence that exists not only for the particular subject who is making the statements but also for others who are paying attention to what is meant. The meant is present for any observer as fulfillment of what is aimed at in intending. The meant refers to what is for the whole, to anyone who might be paying attention to the evidence, and does not refer just to what is present for the individual describing and making the statements. Husserl saw this. Through mathematics we too become aware not only of the number continuum, but also of ourselves and others who likewise exist in a continuum of meaning which is infinite.

The mathematical also involves the psychological. In a study of the psychological significance of medieval alchemy, Jung mentions Leibniz and his view of whole and part. Jung compares that view of Leibniz to a view of the alchemist:

> The alchemist, however, had at the very least an indirect inkling of it: he knew definitely that as part of the whole he had an image of the whole in himself, the "firmament" or "Olympus," as Paracelsus calls it. This interior microcosm was the unwitting object of alchemical research.
>
> (Jung 1979: 164)

Thus, in terms of alchemy, the whole is the firmament, the heavenly, that which is beyond the individual. And yet, the whole also exists somehow in the individual, the earthly. The whole must then be transfinite, for such equivalence between whole and part does not exist in finite wholes. The concept "transfinite number" is thus important psychologically insofar as it makes evident that there is indeed something beyond the individual, something that is not just "heavenly" as beyond, but is also "earthly" as involving everyone else. It is the psychological task of a lifetime to discover and express the individual symbol of the whole that lies latent or "unconscious" in the dim margins of one's awareness. This task belonging to the individual comes from the sense of the whole which itself aims to be expressed in an infinite variety of ways; it compels the notice of the individual and demands constant attention.

For Leibniz, Husserl, and Cantor, the meaning of the infinite is given as a concept. The actuality of the infinite series of infinite series, however, is not given in its fullness. Indeed, the concept is at the same time a symbol for what is not given directly. Husserl affirms that the givenness of this concept, as Idea in the Kantian sense, does not mean that infinity itself is fully given; then he adds that "the insight that this infinity is intrinsically incapable of being given does not exclude but rather demands the transparent givenness of the Idea of this infinity." (Husserl 1958: 398) Infinity is given inadequately as an Idea, as a pure concept of the understanding that transcends the limits of our experience. The concept of "transfinite whole" is at the basis of mathematical study of the number continuum; it is crucial in the philosophical distinction of part and whole; and it clarifies the psychological task of being oneself in relation to others. The significance of this concept is not only thought, but may also be felt, imagined, and hoped for.

Jung would agree with Husserl in affirming that what cannot be given adequately is nevertheless given as an Idea which is both a concept for what is grasped in a limited way and a symbol for what is beyond grasping. Jung would add that this Idea bears tremendous energy and demands expression; he himself was compelled all his life to pay close attention to symbols, dreams, images, concepts, and other kinds of phenomena that indicate what is beyond them. Jung had to pay attention; otherwise, he was not able to live in this world.

# Chapter 9

# Transfinite number as limit and essence

As Jung says, following Paracelsus the alchemist, each individual who discovers "an image of the whole in himself" is discovering at the same time what is equivalent in all individuals, what is there as possible for all and is not said of just one individual. "The whole" that an image symbolizes is not a private possession, but is rather a lived sense in the dim margins of any awareness.

Jung notes that there is an alchemical transformation or psychological achievement when an individual becomes aware of self as bearing some sense of "the whole." Such a sense contains potentially an infinite series of predicates that correspond to predicates in all other individuals, even though an individual cannot enumerate or follow up all the correspondences explicitly. But even a dim awareness of the infinite whole changes a person insofar as it shows the individual that he or she is inexorably connected, to some others directly and to all the rest indirectly.

Ancient stories of creation symbolize such psychological transformation in an individual. In teaching introductory philosophy courses, I included creation myths and used the research of Marie-Louise von Franz, Jung's distinguished collaborator, and particularly her book, *Patterns of Creativity Mirrored in Creation Myths*. My students especially liked ancient stories about the separation of the original whole into Heaven and Earth. An original egg begins to crack and needs effort in being pushed apart; it splits into Father Sky and Mother Earth, freeing a space in between where children may grow. Sometimes tree roots of Heaven still hang in the air or cling onto the edges of cliffs in the newly aerated Earth. (Von Franz 1972: 153–4) Students drew dramatic pictures of the cracking, the pushing, the splitting, and the hanging tree roots. I dreamed last night about such tree roots, with clods of dirt still attached to them, now lodged at a cliff top. Roots up so high gave me the creeps, and I was afraid of the edge. It was like looking down into the infinite series of infinite series.

With the separation of the two halves of the primal egg, however, there is space for the children of Father Sky and Mother Earth to grow. Jung and von Franz maintain that psychological development of an individual requires a symbolic separating that is an actual conscious distinguishing of one's relation to all from one's individual life. A sense of what is more than oneself, a correspondence to a whole, gives great significance to an individual, as each discovers her or his own unique essence or individual concept and takes responsibility for living it out as an irreplaceable expression of the whole.

Once again we recognize the importance of studying the concept of "transfinite number," because the interdependence and equivalence of part and whole cannot be distinguished without some understanding of the infinite, insofar as the equivalence of part and whole does not exist in finite aggregates. The concept of the infinite now requires further clarification through Cantor's definition of "transfinite number."

Let us then approach this definition, which was familiar to Husserl, Cantor's colleague at Halle. In order to understand it, we must again make clear the difference between finite aggregates and transfinite aggregates. We follow Cantor as he states theorem C: "C. Every finite aggregate E is such that it is equivalent to none of its parts." (Cantor 1955: 108) He then makes a distinction, saying: "This theorem stands sharply opposed to the following one for transfinite aggregates: D. Every transfinite aggregate T is such that it has parts $T_1$ which are equivalent to it." (Cantor 1955: 108) Cantor then proves this theorem D, making it clearly evident that transfinite aggregates are not finite aggregates, as each transfinite aggregate has parts equivalent to itself while the finite ones do not. With a crack and a groan, the transfinite splits away as clearly distinct from the finite. We glimpse the difference, but tend to draw away from seeing more: the infinite series of infinite series is dizzying.

A "transfinite number" is a definitely infinite number, and Cantor had discovered them many years before he actually spoke of them publicly. "I was led to them [these numbers] many years ago, without arriving at a clear consciousness that I possessed in them concrete numbers of real significance," he says in an article published in 1883. (Cantor 1955: 53–4) But in 1871, he already had had what he calls a *Vorstellung* or presentation of a transfinite ordinal number, as a definitely infinite order. (Cantor 1955: 32n) Yet, he did not refer to it publicly even in 1880, nine years after the first glimpse. (Cantor 1955: 36n) At the edge of the cliff, where the transfinite was being distinguished from the finite, Cantor was apparently stunned. It took him some time to describe the transfinite numbers clearly, though he felt compelled to do so.

Cantor says:

> I was logically forced, almost against my will ... to the thought of considering the infinitely great, not merely in the form of the unlimitedly increasing ... but also to fix it mathematically by numbers in the definite form of a 'completed infinite'.
>
> (Cantor 1955: 53)

Thus, Cantor slowly came to define—to speak definitely about, in a mathematical way—the transfinite numbers. He repeatedly looked to the evident fact that there is no greatest finite number: supposing that there is such a number leads to contradiction, for we could always add 1 to such a supposed number, and then "the greatest finite number" would not be "the greatest finite number." The series of finite numbers is infinite, not finite. How then can this series be numbered or grasped in a concept?

The series of finite numbers is not finite, in the sense that it has no end or "limit," according to the first sense of the ancient Greek word "limit" as Aristotle defines it in his *Metaphysics* 1022a 4–5: " 'Limit' means (1) the last point of each thing, i.e. the first point beyond which it is not possible to find any part, and the first point within which every part is." (Aristotle, trans. 1941: 770) The series of finite numbers has no limit in this sense. For it has no last point—no last finite number. It has no first finite number beyond which it is not possible to find any more finite numbers. And it does not have a first finite number within which every finite number is. Thus, the series of finite numbers does not have a limit, in this first sense of the word.

There are, however, other senses of the ancient word "limit" as Aristotle distinguishes them in *Metaphysics* 1022a 5–13:

> (2) the form, whatever it may be, of a spatial magnitude or of a thing that has magnitude; (3) the end of each thing (… i.e. the final cause); (4) the substance of each thing, and the essence of each; for this is the limit of knowledge; and if of knowledge, of the object also. Evidently, therefore, 'limit' has as many senses as 'beginning', and yet more; for the beginning is a limit, but not every limit is a beginning.
>
> (Aristotle, trans. 1941: 770)

The series of finite numbers does not have a limit in the second sense of the word, either, for the series is not a spatial magnitude. But the series does have a limit in the sense of end or "final cause" (3), as found in its essence (4), what it is, its *eidos*, its defining order or rule. A limit or essence is what a thing is, as determination and definition of the thing. The essence of the series of finite numbers is the limit or rule by which it is constituted, the form that determines it; by this form, rule, or limit, the series is what it is. The essence is thus both the end towards which the series aims and its origin, insofar as the essence is the limitation or determination by which it is exactly what it is and is not what it is not. Now, the end or "final cause" (3) of a thing is also its essence, insofar as the thing aims to be what it is. The concept of a transfinite number is thus a limit in both senses (4) and (3) insofar as it is the rule originating the series, limiting it to be what it is, defining its essence, and drawing it to its end or final goal of being what it is. The concept "transfinite number" is the essence of the series of the finite numbers as a unitary whole.

So, when Cantor discovered "transfinite number" as a unitary whole, as a general concept of the infinite series of finite numbers, he discovered their limit in the sense of their essence as both their origin and their end. Like Leibniz, Cantor saw that an essence, as concept of a unitary whole, could include an infinite series of elements or predicates, even as uncounted, merely as implicit.

High school students today are familiar with the term "limit" in mathematics. They recognize, for example, that the upper limit of the infinite series of numbers between 2 and 3 is the number 3. For 3 includes, or is constituted by, all that comes before it; it is the first whole number *after* the infinite series which it includes. Accordingly, the limit of the infinite series of all finite numbers, ordered in any way at all, is a limit in the same way: it is "the *first after* all the finite numbers." The first number after all the finite numbers is the first, least non-finite or "transfinite number."

Like most mathematicians of his time, Cantor used letters of our alphabet to name aggregates and letters of the Greek alphabet to name numbers. In a new step, he selected the first letter of the Hebrew alphabet, *aleph*, which the inside back cover of a dictionary says is "often not represented in transliteration," (Stein 1984) to name the least transfinite cardinal number, which is "the *first after* all the finite numbers." Cantor gave it the subscript zero, and so the name "Aleph sub-zero" looks like this: "$\aleph_0$".

$\aleph_0$, the least transfinite "cardinal" number, is the concept of the series as a whole in any order at all, its essence in the abundant sense of the term—the determination, or end, or origin of what all the numbers in the series of finite numbers are together—and it is "the *first after* all the finite numbers," just as 3 is the first after the infinite series of numbers between 2 and 3. Both $\aleph_0$ and 3 are limits, each respectively of its infinite series, as each is not in the series but just beyond the series while determining what the series is as a whole.

The first, least, transfinite "ordinal" number, however, is distinct from $\aleph_0$ insofar as its elements are ordered, and Cantor calls it "$\omega$," *omega*, the last letter of the Greek alphabet in lower case. $\omega$ adds to the concept of $\aleph_0$ the concept of the ordinal rank of its elements, their ordinal type, the order in which they occur. Nonetheless, both the cardinal number $\aleph_0$ and the ordinal number $\omega$ are limits of the series of finite numbers, insofar as both are "first after" or "just beyond" the series. The ordinal number just has the determination of order of elements that the cardinal number does not have: "1, 2, 3, ..., $\nu$, ..., " (where "$\nu$" means "any number that is a positive integer"). In this formula, we see the rule that shows the essence or limit of the series as ordered. Cantor affirms that it is possible to think of $\omega$ as

> the *limit* to which the numbers $\nu$ strive, if by that nothing else is understood than that $\omega$ is to be the first integer which follows all the numbers $\nu$, that is to say, is to be called greater than every $\nu$.
>
> (Cantor 1955: 56–7n)

$\omega$ is thus the unitary concept of the series of finite numbers as an ordered whole, but it is beyond the finite numbers as the first "transfinite ordinal number." In this way, a "transfinite number" is indeed a limit without being "the last finite number."

An examination or enumeration of each element of an infinite series is not required in order to have a general concept or essence of the things in the series because the essence is a "law" or "rule," or sometimes "order of succession," of the things, by which they are what they are. An essence is not a generalization from many particulars, with an expectation that some new particular in the series might turn up as completely different from the others or unrelated to them. Rather, an essence is a rule or necessary statement about the dependence or "non-independence" of the parts or elements in the series. In the series of positive integers, for example, 3 is impossible without 4, 4 is impossible without 3, and each integer is non-independent of all the others. They all exist as a continuum; together they fulfill "what it is to be a positive integer." All are covered by their limit, $\omega$, a transfinite ordinal number. The limit gives their order or rule of dependence, "1, 2, 3, ..., $v$, ...," as their essence, such that one element cannot exist without the others which help make it be what it is, without which it cannot be. The essence expresses the necessary interdependence of all the parts or elements constituting the aggregate. We study the infinite by looking to the limit, the essence, the *eidos* as a whole that is inadequately given.

We can also study the infinite for a few minutes by looking down into the infinite series of infinite series, which I have avoided doing because I get dizzy and scared. Let us first of all get a good hold onto the edge of the abyss by observing the solidity of the proof that $\aleph_0$ exists as limit towards which the finite numbers converge. Philip E. B. Jourdain, who translated Cantor's *Contributions to the Founding of the Theory of Transfinite Numbers* into English and wrote the Introduction, praises Weierstrass's theory, upon which Cantor's theory depends. For, "with Weierstrass, the new numbers [limits] were aggregates of the numbers previously defined," and so there is an important advantage, namely, "that the *existence* of limits can be proved in such a theory." (Cantor 1955: 20) $\aleph_0$ and the other transfinite numbers are based on numbers that were previously shown to exist and are introduced with proper definitions, not merely "as 'creations of our minds,' or, what is far worse, as 'signs,'" through which existence cannot be proved. (Cantor 1955: 20)

Thus, in grasping the concept "transfinite number" as a limit or rule, we are experiencing true actuality, the objectivity of the first least transfinite ordinal number in relation to the finite numbers we have long lived with. The new number is their whole. It is a surprise for us to find out that the finite numbers do make a whole. What is more surprising, and even uncanny, is that there is also an infinite series of numbers between any two given numbers. Moreover, $\aleph_0$ is the first in a series of $\aleph$s; each is a limit, but each limit is also surpassed, just as $\aleph_0$ is surpassed. We go on and on.

After defining $\aleph_0$, Cantor went on to the higher cardinal numbers and showed that they proceed from $\aleph_0$ and that they "can be arranged according to their magnitude, and, in this order, form, like the finite numbers, a 'well-ordered aggregate' in an extended sense of the words." (Cantor 1955: 109) The unlimited sequence of transfinite cardinal numbers $\aleph_0$, $\aleph_1$, $\aleph_2$, ..., $\aleph_v$, ..., goes on without having a greatest transfinite cardinal number. Yet, as Cantor goes on to show, there exists "a cardinal number which we denote by $\aleph_\omega$ and which shows itself to be the next greater to all the numbers $\aleph_\nu$," and out of it there is a next greater and a next greater, and so on, proceeding according to a unitary law, without end. (Cantor 1955: 109)

In providing a rigorous foundation for this matter, Cantor refers to the theory of "ordinal types." A definite ordinal type, or "definite type" for short, is the concept of the order of precedence of elements in an aggregate, without regard to the nature of the elements themselves. Thus, an ordinal type is an ordered aggregate whose elements have the same order as the elements in the aggregate from which they are abstracted. (Cantor 1955: 109–12) Earlier, we noticed that the aggregates of the positive even integers, the positive odd integers, the negative even integers, and the negative odd integers are equivalent. When elements of these aggregates are put in order of increasing or decreasing magnitude, we affirm that the aggregates have the same ordinal type. Cantor finds that the ordinal types of finite ordered aggregates are not interesting. But he finds that the transfinite ordinal types are quite interesting, "for to one and the same cardinal number belong innumerably many different types of simply ordered aggregates, which, in their totality, constitute a particular 'class of types' (*Typenclasse*)." (Cantor 1955: 113–14) The ordinal types that belong to a given cardinal number thus make up a "class of types." Cantor examines these types in detail at length. In the end, he and Jourdain affirm that "every cardinal number is either an Aleph or is greater than all Alephs." (Cantor 1955: 206) They also affirm that "the supposition that a cardinal number is greater than all Alephs is impossible." (Cantor 1955: 206) It seems to follow "that no cardinal number can be other than an Aleph." (Cantor 1955: 206)

In applying "the cardinal number of all things" to an 1892 argument of Cantor, Bertrand Russell, however, found a contradiction involving the concept of an Aleph as a class of ordinal types and the supposition that the number of all things has to be an Aleph as cardinal number. (At this point, I wonder, do "all the things altogether" have a number? Do they even constitute a class?) In any case, Russell indicated that, if the number of all things is an Aleph as cardinal number, then this Aleph, since it is a thing, is a member of its own class. Thus, it is a so-called "non-normal" class, since a "normal" class is one that is not a member of itself. But there is a difficulty with both non-normal classes and normal classes.

Nagel and Newman explain the difficulty rather clearly. If N stands for the class of all normal classes, then we can ask whether N is normal or non-normal. If it is normal, then it belongs in the class of all normal classes. But then it contains itself and so is non-normal. If it is non-normal, it is a member of itself, by definition of non-normal. But then N is also normal because, by definition of N, the members of N are normal classes. "In short, N is normal if, and only if, N is non-normal." (Nagel and Newman 1958: 24)

Jourdain summarizes Russell's contradiction succinctly: "If $w$ is the class of all those terms $x$ such that $x$ is not a member of $x$, then, if $w$ is a member of $w$, it is plain that $w$ is not a member of $w$; while if $w$ is not a member of $w$, it is equally plain that $w$ is a member of $w$." (Cantor 1955: 206) No one can say anything further at this point. Russell's paradox is like the logical puzzle known as "the Epimenides." Epimenides was a Cretan who affirmed that "all Cretans are liars." Thus, if his affirmation is true, he, as a Cretan, is a liar, and what he is saying is not true. (Cantor 1955: 206–7)

Russell, as I noted earlier, for most of his life sought to clear away the indeterminate; he said, "I like precision. I like sharp outlines. I hate misty vagueness." (Russell 1961: 30) Like Epimenides, he stopped the conversation short. He did not put up with a sense of the transfinite whole as going on and on. Rather, he thought of the whole, the "number" of all things, as a class that either had itself as a member or did not. To him it neither made sense that the whole was a member of itself, nor did it make sense that the whole was not a member of itself. So he abandoned the matter as foggy.

Cantor, however, continued on with what he saw in partial clarity, as the existing series of Alephs hovered near, haunted, and even terrified him. He was obsessed with transfinite numbers for years and repeatedly examined them as a problem. Their objective actuality arose before him and filled him with awe. He wrote:

> … in the successive formation of number-classes, we can always go farther, and never reach a limit that cannot be surpassed, – so that we never reach an even approximate comprehension (*Erfassen*) of the Absolute, – I cannot doubt. The Absolute can only be recognized (*anerkannt*), but never apprehended (*erkannt*), even approximately…. The state of things is like that described by Albrecht von Haller: "ich zieh' sie ab [die ungeheure Zahl] (*sic*) und Du [die Ewigkeit] (*sic*) liegst ganz vor mir." ["I take you away, oh monstrous number, and You, Eternity, lie right in front of me."]
>
> (Cantor 1955: 62n)

Moreover, Cantor said that the infinite sequence of counting numbers appeared to him "as a vanishing nothing" in comparison with "the absolutely infinite sequence" of transfinite numbers, the continuing series of Alephs, which seemed to him "to be, in a certain sense, a suitable symbol of the Absolute." (Cantor 1955: 62n)

Cantor had been born in St. Petersburg, Russia, and was an outstanding violinist. He had bouts of depression and anxiety, especially when challenged by colleagues about aspects of his founding of the theory of transfinite numbers, or when his youngest son died suddenly, or when the Great War came. He took the infinite very seriously: like Albrecht von Haller, he addressed it as *Du*, "You" in the personal intimate mode of address in German, rather than *Sie,* the more formal mode. (Cantor 1955: 62n) He died in a sanatorium. (Dauben 1979: 271–99) His response to what he called "transfinite" was quite different from Russell's.

Another possible response to the infinite as surpassing every limit is the one shown by Victor Hugo in his presentation of monseigneur Bienvenu, a kind, generous character in *Les Misérables*. This "Monsignor Welcome" invites to his supper table a newly released prisoner whom no one else in town will admit. When later the prisoner sneaks out into the night with his host's silver candle-sticks, is subsequently caught, and is returned to the host, Bienvenu says that the candlesticks were not stolen but rather given to his guest. Bienvenu thus enables Jean Valjean to feel sorry a short time later, to weep, and to be truly free. The rest of the lengthy story is about the extraordinary life that Valjean then leads. Bienvenu continues to walk in his garden under the night sky, contemplating the stars. Hugo describes him:

> *Il songeait à la grandeur et à la présence de Dieu; à l'éternité future, étrange mystère; à l'éternité passée, mystère plus étrange encore; à tous les infinis qui s'enfonçaient sous ses yeux dans tous les sens; et, sans chercher à comprendre l'incompréhensible, il le regardait. Il n'étudiait pas Dieu, il s'en éblouissait.*

(Hugo 1995: 101)

These words may be translated: He was thinking of the greatness and the presence of God; of future eternity, strange mystery; of past eternity, stranger mystery still; of all the infinities that were sinking before his eyes in every direction; and, without seeking to comprehend the incomprehensible, he was looking at it. He was not studying God; he was becoming dazzled with God.

# Chapter 10

# Subjectivity

Future eternity, strange mystery; past eternity, stranger mystery still. Husserl too became dazzled with the infinite, even as he studied it repeatedly. Focusing on the infinite in the streaming phenomena of awareness, he saw a "double continuity of time-consciousness," and sketched the presence of the past and the future in the present as two perpendicular co-ordinated lines. The two lines symbolize a double continuity as a whole whose originating center bears a likeness to (0,0), the origin of all the points and lines on a graph. In the originating center, Husserl saw the origin of subjective experience in which appearances of anything arise. In and from each new moment as a center, appearances arise afresh as a new phase of time and a new phase of subjective experiencing. If there were no continually new "now" holding the doubly continuous past and future, then no experience, no appearing, no presence of anything at all would be possible. But there is continually a new "now" in which there is double continuity. This continually new presence, Husserl writes in paragraph 36 of *The Phenomenology of Internal Time-Consciousness*, is "a point of actuality, primal source point, that from which springs the 'now,' and so on." (Husserl 1964: 100) But he adds: "For all this, names are lacking." (Husserl 1964: 100)

This "that from which" has nevertheless been noticed by others like Cantor or Hugo, who called it "the Eternal" as persistent presence of the now with its infinities of future and past. It has also been called "Absolute" as depended upon by all that is relative to it. As origin of subjective experience, Husserl refers to it as the incomprehensible depth of subjectivity. Jung calls it "the Self" in the ancient Hindu sense of *Ātman*, as found in the Katha Upanisad. (Jung 1976a: 124; 1976b: 198) In this Upanisad, Death is instructing a young man named Naciketas, whom Death praises: "Thou art not one who has taken that garland of wealth/ In which many men sink down." (Radhakrishnan 1957: 45) Then Death continues his instruction:

> The wise one [i.e., the *Ātman*, the Self] (*sic*) is not born, nor dies.
> This one has not come from anywhere, has not become anyone.
> Unborn, constant, eternal, primeval, this one
> Is not slain when the body is slain....

More minute than the minute, greater than the great,
Is the Self that is set in the heart of a creature here....
The great, all-pervading Self – ...

(Radhakrishnan 1957: 45–6)

Higher than the Unmanifest is the Person.
Higher than the Person there is nothing at all....

(Radhakrishnan 1957: 47)

He who is awake in those that sleep,
The Person who fashions desire after desire – ...
As the one fire has entered the world
And becomes corresponding in form to every form,
So the one Inner Self (*antarātman*) of all things
Is corresponding in form to every form, and yet is outside.

(Radhakrishnan 1957: 48)

Husserl seems to have had a similar sense of "Self" when he was writing about subjectivity in the following radical yet puzzling way:

It is a realm of something subjective which is completely closed off within itself, existing in its own way, functioning in all experiencing, all thinking, all life, thus everywhere inseparably involved; yet it has never been held in view, never been grasped and understood.

(Husserl 1970a: 112)

How can something be "completely closed off within itself," yet at the same time be "everywhere inseparably involved"? How can it be "functioning in all experiencing, all thinking, all life," but never be "held in view ... grasped and understood"? Husserl studies "the greatest of the great" by repeatedly observing "the smallest of the small," the moments of consciousness as they pass in time.

To begin an analysis of time-consciousness with Husserl is to turn our attention to our living experience as we are living it, and explicitly to notice now that it is experience in time. Whatever else is happening during a given experience, we have at least this much: a lived sense of passing and enduring. As we become more aware of our ongoing awareness itself, other objects fall into the background of attention. For example, I was preparing potatoes and cabbage a few minutes ago, and then I put them on the stove in a pot. Then they were occupying the foreground of my attention. Now as I write, they are not my primary focus; rather, my interest now is in basic aspects of awareness—how it passes, how it retains, how it continues on—another kind of objectivity altogether. My awareness of cooking does not cease to be an awareness about cooking, but the aspect of cooking becomes secondary now as I turn my attention primarily to that awareness *as* awareness, particularly in its temporal aspects of passing and enduring. I am now making up for times when I neglected awareness, times when the cooking interest was primary and the study of awareness was secondary.

During the passing and enduring that we notice in our experiencing, we can distinguish what Husserl calls "transcendence" and "immanence." Experience is transcendent insofar as it makes what exists beyond us temporally present to us; experience gives me the other, the not fully known, the abundance around me as well as myself. But at the same time, experience is immanent, for in every case experience is "mine." It necessarily belongs to, in, and with a "me." A thoroughly individual, personally lived experiencing provides the genuine presence of a transcendent object. This means that objective time, the time of spatio-temporal reality or world-history, is indeed transcendent, objective, and genuine, but is so *through being meant and given* in modes of immanent subjective experiencing. The experiencing in which transcendence acquires temporal presence is itself interesting to study, or look at, or at least glimpse.

We often confuse transcendence and immanence, like a red-haired five-year-old girl I knew many years ago. Visiting us, she was wearing thick new eyeglasses. "I have to wear these," she explained with great enthusiasm, "because look what happens when I take them off." She naïvely expected us to see her visual field as directly as she was seeing it; she identified her immanent event with its transcendent objectivity. In some ways she was right, however, for we did feel and imagine what she was seeing. But she did not yet know our perspectives. So her sense of transcendent objectivity as "what is there for anyone" was not abundant. Years of experience since then have developed her sense of transcendence in relation to immanence.

We now look at awareness as passing, enduring, and immanent, despite whatever transcendent objectivity it may be making present. We notice that apparently simple acts of sense perception are a continual, spontaneous, yet individual achievement, an immanent process that only gradually gives an ever more meaningful presence of an objective world. Sensation requires some kind of receptivity and expectation. It needs memory, recognition, and relation as modes of subjective intending in order for it to be a genuine perception of something. More fundamentally, sensation is nothing apart from a continual passing and enduring of awareness; sensation exists insofar as it is felt or suffered. It is not a spatial putting of data from outside to inside.

We try to hold time in our notice as passing yet enduring experience, as succession and duration. But time is hard to study. Whatever moment or part of experience we attend to goes right by. It is there only as passing. How then did we even notice it? It must endure since we noticed it. But all that seems to endure is the continuous passing. But how does even that endure? For what has passed by no longer actually exists. What is here now is no sooner here than it is gone. What is about to be does not even exist yet. In a dark moment, nothing seems to actually be here.

Coincidentally, as I began to write early this morning, city workers in trucks marked "Forestry" arrived in the small cemetery across the street. Human remains had long ago been removed from that burial land. Now as I write, the city workers are cutting down, branch by branch, a large sugar maple tree that had endured about 150 years up to this day. And now, a while later, there is a large gap where it used to be. A tree growth of 150 years is now gone, part into large logs that are being removed, and the rest into a shredder. The logs will become ashes when burned as firewood. All passes.

So what endures, and when? Even duration, the *time when* something endures, seems to slip away in the continuous passing of time. The early medieval philosopher Augustine thought deeply and seriously about the passing of time. Husserl turned to Augustine, appreciating him as one "who labored almost to despair over this problem.... For no one in this knowledge-proud modern generation has made more masterful or significant progress in these matters than this great thinker ...." (Husserl 1964: 30) In his *Confessions XI,15*, Augustine says:

> In fact the only time that can be called present is an instant, if we can conceive of such, that cannot be divided even into the most minute fractions, and a point of time as small as this passes so rapidly from the future to the past that its duration is without length. For if its duration were prolonged, it could be divided into past and future. When it is present it has no duration.
>
> (Augustine 1961: 266)

In this sense, the present instant, the only truly actual time, is indivisible and has no duration, no length. Yet, paradoxically, we still feel duration. At this moment, are we not experiencing a length of time, a somehow enduring length of time, whose moments are nevertheless succeeding one another? The passing does endure now. As the succession of moments of time continues, somehow the succession itself is retained in the present moment as "just having been." The succession in its different parts—the future, present, and past moments—is sustained in some way *now*. As Augustine observes in XI, 18, these parts or moments of the succession do continue somehow to exist in the present: "wherever they are and whatever they are, it is only by being present that they *are*." (Augustine 1961: 267) But future, present, and past do not exist in any place or space, not even in "the world in general," inasmuch as they are aspects of temporal, not spatial, extension. Space holds what is simultaneous, all at once, one thing next to another. But time is a continuous succession of phases; strictly speaking, time is nowhere—only *when*. While places in space endure in and for lengths of time, parts of time as successive do not endure anywhere in space.

Experience as immanent is thus somehow an enduring continuity of successive passing. In this continuity, present, past, and future exist and constitute the presence of something transcendent *during each* present phase of living experience. A present moment thus has a fullness that we cannot adequately describe merely by saying it is an instant. For, as Augustine writes in XI, 19–28, any present moment is also simultaneously a *present expectation* of what will come to pass, a *present attention* to what is now passing, and a *present memory* of what has passed. Future, present, and past phases are present in relation to a continuity of expectation, attention, and memory as spontaneous modes of living experience that are continually relating to one another. We can begin to notice the fullness and continuity for ourselves, seeing what we are in a new way. Our time-consciousness is neither arbitrary nor private, nor is it a socially constructed product of an historical period. Rather, it is presupposed in and for any historical period. The most powerful historical forces still need time to exist during. They exist in inseparable relation to succession and duration, to some kind of immanent experiencing, to the fullness of expectation, attention, and memory. They are non-independent of subjectivity.

Succession and duration in living experience can be looked at repeatedly, studied, and symbolized in a diagram, even as the birds sing in the trees, the wind blows, and the vegetables cook on the stove. Through observing, Husserl clarifies how succession and duration are interdependent. He starts with only a small example, following Augustine in XI, 23 who prayed: "O God, grant that men should recognize in some small thing like this potter's wheel the principles which are common to all things, great and small alike." (Augustine 1961: 271) Augustine actually begins with something even more ordinary than a potter's wheel: "a noise emitted by some material body." (Augustine 1961: 275) Then he enlarges this example to the sounding of three words from a hymn: "*Deus Creator omnium.*" At length in chapter 28, he finds that what is true of a whole temporal sounding is true of all its parts, and furthermore, true of any longer temporal whole—a whole life or even the whole history of the human race. (Augustine 1961: 278) It begins, it ends, it sinks into the past.

Like Augustine, Husserl in *The Phenomenology of Internal Time-Consciousness*, paragraph 8, begins with a tone sounding and is looking for some fundamental principle of succession and duration in appearing. He describes in detail how a sound is given for him:

> It begins and stops, and the whole unity of its duration, the unity of the whole process in which it begins and ends, "proceeds" to the end in the ever more distant past…. I can direct my attention to the mode of its being given. I am conscious of the sound and the duration which it fills in a continuity of "modes," in a "continuous flux."
>
> (Husserl 1964: 44)

For me, it is given: *Hmmm.* It begins, it ends, it sinks into the past—and I observe this passing. I notice how it appears now, and then now, and then now. At every new moment, it appears as yet farther past. I see that its "mode" or way of being given is changing continuously. The sound continues to be given in changing modes of "farther past." I am conscious of the sound and its duration, not only as it is sounding, but also after it has sounded, in a continuing flux of modes of appearing. The sound itself is continuously appearing yet in continuously different ways: first as "not yet," then as "now," then as "just past," then as "farther past," and then "still farther past," and so on. It is the way it appears, the temporal mode, the relation to the actual now, that changes continuously, not the tone itself, *Hmmm*.

These modes of appearing belong to any temporal part—to any point, moment, phase, or interval of appearance. The temporal whole of appearing is the continuity of these parts, the inseparability of the moments, insofar as any one can exist only in relation to the others and, reciprocally, insofar as the others cannot exist without it. This interdependence constitutes an enduring character in the continuous passing. For, given any new present moment, the other moments endure and continue to exist in it and in relation to it, as each in its temporal mode is newly suited to the order determined by that new present moment. In each new successive moment, the other moments (the "not yet," or "just past," or "farther past," and so on) are given successively in continuously different ways of appearing that are nevertheless unique for each new moment. A moment in a "not yet" mode of appearing changes its mode into a "now" mode of appearing, and then into a "just past" mode, and then into "farther past," and so on into darkness. But any temporal moment of appearing is present in some mode insofar as it is a possibly appearing part of the continuity that is the present moment "now," which is itself a part of the successive continuity.

Each present moment itself contains a continuity, besides the continuity of succession it is part of. For each present moment gives a new temporal relation to the other moments; in relation to that given present moment, each of the others is "not yet," or "just past," or "farther past," and so on, in specific ways. Each moment has its own change of appearing modes for all the other moments. Each new "now" has its own unique "take" (or maybe "give" is a better description) on all the others according to the order in which it holds them. The new continuity in each new moment constitutes the enduring character in each successively new moment. Let us look again for ourselves. Is there a new moment now? Yes. Did I make it happen? No. Is there a new relation of modes of appearance in it? Yes. Does a modified continuity of moments appear successively in each of the succeeding moments? Yes. Thus, the present moment is not a dimensionless instant, but is rather a continuously changing continuity of moments of future and past, even as it is continuously replaced by a new moment which contains its own shifts of the successive continuity. The presence of such continuity *within* the succession of new moments makes up a *double* continuity of succession and duration in living experience that is immanent yet that simultaneously makes possible the presence of anything transcendent.

Accordingly, a new moment is like a transfinite number, not only insofar as it is a unit in an infinite succession of units, but also insofar as it has parts that are equivalent to itself. An article by Thomas M. Seebohm, "Reflexion and Totality in the Philosophy of E. Husserl," in the *Journal of the British Society for Phenomenology* many years ago turned my attention to the transfinite character of the present moment. Each new moment contains an order of moments that is unique in its relations of the various temporal modes of appearing (as future, present, past, farther past, etc.). Each moment happens only once and is irreplaceable, just as each number is. Moreover, each new moment contains an infinite series that is equivalent to the whole succession—not equal to it, but in one-to-one correspondence with it. Each new present moment is a whole, a limit that contains an infinite series of parts which are also moments containing an infinite series of parts. The parts are thus equivalent to the whole they are part of. We are falling into the infinite series of infinite series again, and are becoming dizzy if not dazzled.

Let us then try to focus on Husserl's apparently simple diagram for the double continuity we have been describing. (Husserl 1966: 28) AE represents the line of succession of now moments. AA' represents the sinking down of a moment into the mode of "just past" in a subsequent moment; PP' represents a parallel sinking down of another moment. EA' represents the now point with its horizon of the past as a continuum of points. E in the bottom part, with its arrow pointing ahead, represents the line of succession as open to being fulfilled by the experience of other objects. The second part indicates a continuation of the first; in effect, both parts make one diagram.

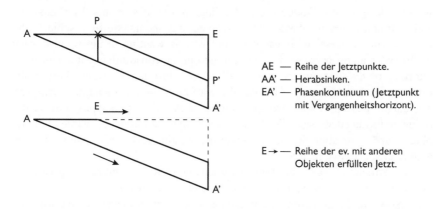

AE — Reihe der Jetztpunkte.
AA' — Herabsinken.
EA' — Phasenkontinuum (Jetztpunkt mit Vergangenheitshorizont).

E→ — Reihe der ev. mit anderen Objekten erfüllten Jetzt.

Husserl's mathematical drawing represents the present moment by both a point P and two straight lines perpendicular at P. It suggests that, at each point P along any given line AE of temporal succession, there is not only a dimensionless point P, but also a straight line perpendicular to AE at P that can be extended indefinitely at either end, even though the line is drawn as ending. The point and the perpendicular lines suggest that a present moment is simultaneously both an indivisible instant and an enduring continuum that is carried along as a new vertical line *in* each new horizontal point, a vertical line that extends up to the open future and down to the past, just as P extends horizontally on AE towards the open future with its past.

Moreover, in the successive series of moments, a present moment is like a number inasmuch as each has precisely one point in an ordered line. Each number has its place in the line of ordinal numbers; each present moment has its unique place in the temporal order of before and after. As a number is a limit of an infinite series before it—the way 3 contains the infinite series between 2 and 3—so a present moment is also a limit, insofar as it is a whole that contains an infinite series—the continuum of past and future. Each new present moment successively contains the successive continuum, the vertical line of past below and future above, with corresponding modes for each of its moments newly coordinated to the present moment. Thus, a second infinite series is continually a part of each new moment of the first series to which it is equivalent; each successive vertical line *is* the horizontal line *in continuously different modes of appearing* in relation to each new P. Each new vertical line is a new way for the horizontal line to appear—as farther past for each new P. This double continuity of succession and duration in living experience cannot be understood without understanding how an infinite series can be equivalent to the whole of which it is a part. For no finite series can be equivalent to the whole of which it is a part. The depth of subjectivity, the unseen origin of succession and duration, involves the transfinite, even though we cannot count all the moments of time.

Ironically, Husserl's diagram is dead without the presence of a living observer who is taking time to notice time. The diagram clarifies temporal instantaneity and continuity only insofar as it is perceived and understood by a subject who is perceiving successive appearances and who is wanting to notice successive duration. To an observer who is not seeking out the constitutive features of time, the parts of the diagram are present all at once in relation to one another; the lines are not continuously changing the way moments of a sounding tone are. The diagram as a purely formal spatial figure lacks what it is supposed to clarify: living enduring succession. For figures are eternal, "all at once," while temporal objects are "one after the other," enduring continuously only insofar as they endure in successive phases.

It nevertheless amazes me that this unchanging formal figure can give me a clearer sense of double continuity than the one I had when I was just hearing the tone. Now I find that it continues to engage my attention in an affective way that Husserl probably did not intend: I am finding something funny in it. As I stare at it, the diagram of dynamic time reminds me of Plato's description in *Timaeus* 37d of time as "a moving image of eternity." (Plato, trans. 1963: 1167) Eternity is absolute stillness, all present all at once, "immovably the same forever," he writes in 38a. (Plato, trans. 1963: 1167) Time is supposedly *like* this; it is the *image* of motionlessness—except, of course, for the fact that it *moves*. Is this a joke, an instance of Socratic irony and pathos? But the context of this saying about time is sublime: it is a creation myth, as we see in 37c–e:

> When the father and creator saw the creature which he had made moving and living, the created image of the eternal gods, he rejoiced, and in his joy determined to make the copy still more like the original, and as this was an eternal living being, he sought to make the universe eternal, so far as might be. Now

the nature of the ideal being was everlasting, but to bestow this attribute in its fullness upon a creature was impossible. Wherefore he resolved to have a moving image of eternity, and when he set in order the heaven, he made this image eternal but moving according to number, while eternity itself rests in unity, and this image we call time.

(Plato, trans. 1963: 1167)

Time moves according to number yet is eternal. Time and eternity are radically different yet inseparable, in ways I cannot comprehend. Is the unchanging diagram then an unmoving image of time? Is it just like time except for the fact that it lacks succession? But if it lacks succession, then how can it be like time, insofar as time is successive duration? The diagram tears me up, as I see through it that life in its actual presence at this moment is my access to both time and eternity.

The now moment is always presupposed as enduring, yet it is not apparent as a spatial object. It appears as a self-relating double continuity. It thus coincides with what Husserl says in a quotation, made at the beginning of this essay, about *subjectivity* as, on one hand, inseparably involved "in all experiencing, all thinking, all life," yet simultaneously as, on the other hand, "completely closed off within itself" in the sense that it does not itself appear as a thing. (Husserl 1970a: 112) The actual present is presupposed in all experiencing, thinking, and life, insofar as they cannot exist without it. At the same time, the actual now as new is closed off in the sense that it does not exist anywhere as a spatial object, even though it is inseparably involved in all spatial appearing. The essential character of time is distinct, unique, and irreducible to any spatial thing. In examining time, we are necessarily in the presence of subjectivity, the "subjective realm" so important to Husserl that he could not name it.

Successive duration is no dead mechanical process occurring somehow spatially, as if completely independent from subjects who live, feel, expect, and retain. It is nothing apart from some actual suffering, undergoing, or enduring that one is subjected to or put under, in the sense of the Latin word *subiectus*. (Kidd 1961: 319) Subjectivity is the bearing of experience, as being under, near, or exposed to experience. Subjectivity is an individual ability to be impressed by objects, to be responsive to whatever is present, and to engage in what draws one's attention. Subjectivity is neither reducible to some particular action, like hearing or seeing, nor is it some particular object, like a tone or the soup. Husserl finds himself at a loss in trying to describe radical subjectivity much further. He writes in paragraph 36 of *The Phenomenology of Internal Time-Consciousness*:

We can only say that this flux is something which we name in conformity with what is constituted, but it is nothing temporally "Objective." It is absolute subjectivity and has the absolute properties of something to be denoted metaphorically as "flux," as a point of actuality, primal source-point, that from which springs the "now," and so on. In the lived experience of actuality, we have the primal source-point and a continuity of moments of reverberation .... For all this, names are lacking.

(Husserl 1964: 100)

Yet Husserl calls the flux of the new now "absolute subjectivity." It is "absolute" in the sense that it is what all that is relative relates to, inasmuch as "absolute" and "relative" are terms whose meaning is interdependent. In the end, the Absolute depends on the Relative, as it cannot be absolute without the relative. Husserl does not name it, however, any more than Jews name G-d.

# Chapter 11

# Double intentionality in time-consciousness

Let us count 1, 2, 3, ..., v, ... as far as we wish. Let 1 correspond to a phase of silence. Let 2 correspond to the beginning of a tone sounding, 3 to its ending, 4 to a moment just after, 5 to a moment just after that ... and so on. The continuity of our counting thus corresponds to the continuity of the running-off of phases of silence and sounding. But, as we have seen earlier in considering 3 as a limit of the infinite series of numbers between 2 and 3, each integer contains the series of numbers between itself and the preceding integer—all the rational numbers (like $\frac{7}{3}$) and all the irrational numbers (like $\sqrt{5}$). Each integer also includes the previous integers, as part of itself, as necessary for it to be what it is. For what is 3 without 2, or without 1? 2 and 1 are parts necessary to 3. Thus, in our assigning of numbers to moments of time, 2 corresponds to a moment that contains all the moments up to itself, in relation to itself as present. Likewise, 3 corresponds to a moment that contains all the moments up to itself, in relation to itself as present. Then 4 as a new "now" moment includes all that is previous, in relation to itself—and so on. The continuity of running-off of phases of a tone sounding is thus a continuity of moments that continually includes continuities, just as numbers include continuities.

Each now-phase retains the "just past" of the running-off, as modified or "pushed down into the past" in relation to the new present. As each now is changed into a past, writes Husserl in paragraph 10 of *The Phenomenology of Internal Time-Consciousness*, "the entire continuity of the running-off of the pasts of the preceding points moves uniformly 'downward' into the depths of the past." (Husserl 1964: 50) Husserl continues:

> Every actual now of consciousness, however, is subject to the law of modifi-cation. The now changes continuously from retention to retention. There results, therefore, a stable continuum which is such that every subsequent point is a retention for every earlier one. And every retention is already a continuum.
>
> (Husserl 1964: 50–1)

Thus, time, like number, is a continuity of continuities.

After writing these last paragraphs, I am tired and soon go to sleep. I awake at 2:00 a.m., remembering that in my sleep, I was thinking about the Latin words *magister* and *magistrātus*: they were coming up before me, both in meaning and in print. I notice that something in me was wanting to have the right meaning before me, as both correct and elegant, with beauty and simplicity. I think of the Latin word *frūgi*, "frugal, temperate, honest; useful." (Kidd 1961: 141) *Frux, frūgis* in the plural means first of all "fruits of the earth, produce." (Kidd 1961: 142) The farmers and the produce I buy from them later in the morning at the farmers' market are correct, elegant, and frugal—as temperate, honest, and useful. In the dream, something in me was wanting to produce a correct meaning, to put it before me in perception and in print, as though on a stage, with similar frugality. "To put before" in German is *vorstellen*; in Kant's philosophy, *Vorstellung* means what is put before consciousness, a presentation of something to awareness, akin to presentations on a stage. There is an intending toward meaning going on in me, and very early this morning I caught a glimpse of its effort, its going towards something before me, as if putting it together and going through possibilities to get the right one there. I briefly saw and remember an active intending going on of itself, as part of a dream in my sleep, as seeking and looking for just the right thing to aim attention at, arranging and pulling out what is to be there. I awoke slowly with an urgent sense to remember this intending and to try to describe it in words.

Before I went to sleep and had the dream, I had been wondering if what I had written that day was true: does each retention of the "just past" also include memory of the "far, far past," the way a given number includes all the numbers before it? I had gone to sleep hoping I might have a dream that would teach me what to write next. In recording the dream, I thought about the word *magister, -tri*, m., male teacher. I had not been dreaming of the word *magistra, -ae*, f., female teacher, referring to myself as a teacher or to another female Latin teacher I know. Rather, the word had meant "male teacher," which recalls to me the inner teacher Augustine spoke of, the recollection that Plato saw as the core of learning, and the "animus" or spirit in woman that C. G. Jung observed in women around him.

The word *magistrātus, -ūs*, m., magistrate, official, belongs to a different declension and does not mean "teacher," but rather refers to someone who administers a city or state. We read this word in Caesar. The magistrates of the Helvetian state compelled a multitude of men to leave the fields where they were working and come to town, in order to help defend the state from the thousands of people Orgetorix was bringing in as a cover. Orgetorix was in chains for conspiring to overthrow the state; he thought he might escape by bringing thousands of his people into the city as a distraction. He had taken power and had convinced many people to undertake a migration from Helvetia, ancient Switzerland, to the Gallic Province, southern France. The magistrates found him out and were going to burn him at the stake if he were found guilty. He was killed when all the crowds were in the city. We translated Caesar's history of the Helvetian migration that happened over 2,000 years ago. 258,000 people died, not counting the Romans and the Gauls who fought against the migrating tribes. Many more died, as the following six books of Caesar's history attest.

Some of the Gauls survived and were my ancient ancestors. If they had not survived, would I be here today? Or could I have come to be from somebody else, anybody else, or even from a little piece of dust? Could the *eidos* or essence of me have taken up just any materials at all? Does this essence, which is my limit, my end or aim, require a specific beginning, a lineage of parenting, which alone could produce me? Could I be me without having these eyes and this skeleton? My whole life might have been different if I had not had brown eyes and a face like my mother's. Does what I am and have been come from all my ancestors, as a primary source or original cause? I remember seeing my father's mother on her death bed. She was almost 101 years old. She was trying to do something very intently, concentrating on something inside so hard that she hardly noticed I was there. I looked at her head and felt it was Gallic, French, very old in structure, with something there still from the Gauls. I am trying to get these words right, as I did when I was first recording my dream in my journal. This trying to write, to see what comes up of its own accord and tell it accurately, is like the action of the intending in my sleep, the trying to arrange something right, as before me, on a stage. In trying to write I am imitating an action of tending towards a fulfillment of meaning in some kind of perception (including dream perception), an action that is already going on.

The teacher is not the city official. What teaches me is not a public power. Something frugal, akin to the fruits of the soil, arises and intends and puts before me, selects and arranges for me, what is there as present—and does this with an eye for elegance, simplicity, even beauty, although there is so much to each thing there that I begin to imagine that there might be an infinite series of relations of things. Through a dream, I now have an inkling that the far, far past does exist in relation to the present and the recent past; what happened 2,000 years ago has bearing on what I am, even if I can't explicitly tell how.

What, then, is time? It is a continually meant present moment, tending toward the future and retaining a continuity of past moments that are continually modified as "farther past." The ever-new now with its expectation and retention enables us to have phenomena before us, appearances of things and of ourselves, as the surrounding world. Yet our perception does not cause an original now to be given spontaneously, to be there as never having been before. We immediately expect a new moment to be present, but we don't put it there. Neither our expectation nor our memory creates the now-moment upon which both depend. As we watch the future come to pass, we are not sure what will happen. Our expecting, perceiving, and remembering make up our consciousness in time, but they take time to happen. Time as spontaneous origin and temporal order is beyond the lived intentional acts of perceiving, remembering, and expecting; there is another intending that makes the latter intentional acts possible. This other intending is a "double" to them, not as a duplication but rather as a distinct tending toward meaning without which they cannot exist.

Intentional processes, spatial movement, and experienced stillness all depend upon the "flux"—a new original present in constantly modified relation to its open-ended future and its ever-increasing past. Husserl speaks of it in paragraph 34 as "the constitutive flux" because it is the form or essence that constitutes time or makes it be what it is. (Husserl 1964: 98) The essence of time is an ever-new present which "flows" without going more quickly or more slowly. It does not change. It is not a changing object. It holds a continuous "falling back" of past moments and aims towards future moments. It is present as temporal form that is continually being intended.

Transcendent objects, like a tone sounding, appear in successive duration that is immanent. This immanent duration has successive phases in what Husserl calls in paragraph 39 "the form of temporally constitutive consciousness" as its non-independent parts. (Husserl 1964: 109) Indeed, while hearing and remembering the transcendent tone, we were noticing moments of expectation, attention, and retention as phases of consciousness; they too were apparent. We were also noticing that these phases had a formal essential order by which they were and are what they were and are. The tone, the acts of perceiving, and their formal order were present together inseparably. The tone itself was not our primary interest; the awareness in which the tone was apparent and the successive order of retentional modification were. And now we are noticing the formal ordering as itself an intending that enables the acts of perceiving to be what they are. Husserl says in paragraph 39:

> Consequently, like two aspects of one and the same thing, there are in the unique flux of consciousness *two* inseparable, homogeneous *intentionalities* which require one another and are interwoven with one another. By means of the one, immanent time is constituted, i.e., an Objective time, an authentic time in which there is duration and alteration of that which endures. In the other is constituted the quasi-temporal disposition of the phases of the flux, which ever and necessarily has the flowing now-point, the phase of actuality, and the series of pre-actual and post-actual (of the not yet actual) phases. This pre-phenomenal, pre-immanent temporality is constituted intentionally as the form of temporally constitutive consciousness and in the latter itself. The flux of the immanent, temporally constitutive consciousness not only *is*, but is so remarkably and yet so intelligibly constituted that a self-appearance of the flux necessarily subsists in it, and hence the flux itself must necessarily be comprehensible in the flowing. The self-appearance of the flux does not require a second flux, but *qua* phenomenon it is constituted in itself.
>
> (Husserl 1964: 109)

The flux of time-consciousness is so remarkably and intelligibly constituted—indeed, frugally and elegantly so—that it is a double intentionality, simultaneously making something transcendent present and making itself present as a continual forming. For the flux of awareness intends not only the objects beyond itself as present, but also intends its own temporal form: it tends towards a future moment in a new present moment which retains past moments again and again. But we rarely notice the doubly intending flux itself, in favor of the spatial objectivity it makes present. Without the continual intending of the formal temporal order, however, nothing could be present for us.

Something frugal, akin to the fruits of the soil, arises and intends and puts before me, selects and arranges for me, what is there as present—and does this with an eye for elegance, simplicity, even beauty, although there is so much to each thing there that I begin to imagine that there might be an infinite series of relations of things. In any case, there is an infinite series of relations in the temporal order itself. The flux as form of temporally constitutive consciousness is apparent with the objects it makes present, if only we would notice. But sometimes it takes a dream for me to notice.

Is time thus hidden, frozen in a snowdrift? Does it hasten? Is it still? Is an instant big? Do dreams teach us? Do they put presence before our eyes? In his poem, "Anterooms," Richard Wilbur observes:

Out of the snowdrift
Which covered it, this pillared
Sundial starts to lift,

Able now at last
To let its frozen hours
Melt into the past

In bright, ticking drops.
Time so often hastens by,
Time so often stops—

Still, it strains belief
How an instant can dilate,
Or long years be brief.

Dreams, which interweave
All our times and tenses, are
What we can believe:

Dark they are, yet plain,
Coming to us now as if
Through a cobwebbed pane

Where, before our eyes,
All the living and the dead
Meet without surprise.

(Wilbur 2010: 13)

# Part III

# Distinguishing intentional acts

# Chapter 12

# Memory and feeling

Memory and feeling are intentional acts of awareness that often tend toward the subjectivity of another. In this section, my aim is to make them more evident, but not with the help of mathematical or philosophical concepts, which were used above to describe the flow of phenomena as a whole. Now, rather, I attend to what is given in parts of Edith Stein's autobiography as she was remembering and feeling the significance of her life over many years. In paying attention to this written description of experience, I experience memory and feeling, both my own and hers. Attending to the experience of another activates empathy and remembering on the part of the observer that is distinct from, but related to, that of the one observed. Stein's life is particularly characterized by empathy, the awareness of another as other. Her way of remembering is also worthy of notice, as a gathering up of her whole life as though in anticipation of her death. Paying attention to her feeling and remembering as they are given in her written descriptions is a way of noticing the character of these intentional acts, both as she lived them and as we live our own.

Edith Stein showed an unceasing interest in others. She began her autobiography, *Life in a Jewish Family*, with her mother's remembrances, and spoke of her childhood in terms of "the two youngest," Edith and her sister Erna. (Stein 1986: 62) She had begun the work at the suggestion of a priest advisor, (Stein 1986: 464) and her aim was to tell her own experience of Jewish life "as information for anyone wishing to pursue an unprejudiced study from original sources" (Stein 1986: 24) and especially for young people who had been "reared in racial hatred from earliest childhood." (Stein 1986: 24) We have today nearly 400 printed pages of detailed accounts of Stein's experiences with individuals whom life brought in her way. For she held each in memory and continued to feel connected to them all, as she wrote in a letter: "The formation of an unshakable bond with all whom life brings in my way, a bond in no way dependent on day-to-day contact, is a significant element in my life. And you can depend on that .... " (Stein 1993: #38a)

Even when she did not indicate to anyone what she was suffering, as during a time when her health was very poor, "probably as a result of the spiritual conflicts I then endured in complete secrecy and without any human support," she had another kind of support. (Stein 1986: 237) Husserl and Jung might have called it the source-point of consciousness, time, or energy, but for Stein this other became personal, as another intending transcendent to her yet present in the depth of her subjectivity. Her experience reminds me of what Jung spoke of as "a function of relationship to the world of objects, bringing the individual into absolute, binding, and indissoluble communion with the world at large." (Jung 1966: 178)

Stein felt a bond with all whom life brought her way, a communion with the world at large. She wrote her doctoral dissertation under Husserl's direction and chose to examine empathy, an intentional act *sui generis* in which awareness of the awareness of another, as such, is lived. (Stein 1989: 11) The study of feeling was overlooked in Husserl's thought. Stein's work attempted to fill the gap.

Stein's arrival in Göttingen in April, 1913, marked the beginning of her "travel," her being formed over a long period of time. In remembering her student years there and writing about them, she reflects:

> A long, long way lay behind me when I returned to Göttingen once more in March, 1921, nearing the most important decision of my life; it was a way I began to travel that April day of the year 1913 when I had come there for the first time.
>
> (Stein 1986: 239)

The most important decision of her life was to become a contemplative Carmelite nun, which involved her becoming a Catholic. From her words, it is evident that her way to this decision began when she first came to Göttingen in April, 1913. "Dear Göttingen!" she wrote; "I do believe only someone who studied there between 1905 and 1914, the short flowering time of the Göttingen School of Phenomenology, can appreciate all that the name invokes in us." (Stein 1986: 239) Stein met Husserl there for the first time. Phenomenology and the phenomenologists had drawn her; for Stein, the two were inseparable. (Stein 1986: 247)

Stein had left her mother, who worked very hard in her lumberyard all day, was thoroughly fatigued in the evenings, called her bed "the most wonderful place in the world," and had very vivid dreams. (Stein 1986: 59) As Stein's father had died before Edith was two years old, she had slept with her mother until she was six. For her mother, who had given birth to eleven children and seen four die in childhood, the youngest child Edith was "the final legacy from my father." (Stein, 1986: 39) Her mother's need for rest affected Edith even as she was writing her memories; she confided, "When I lift my head from the pillow early in the morning, she is wont to motion me back: 'Wait, wait, there is still plenty of time.'" (Stein 1986: 59) Thus, even after she had left her mother and embarked on the road to becoming a Carmelite nun, the life and warmth of her mother drew her to renewing rest.

Stein's time as a student in Göttingen was interrupted by World War. In April, 1915, she set out for Mährisch-Weisskirchen to be a volunteer nurse for the Red Cross. She kept up a written correspondence with Husserl, whose birthplace, Prossnitz, was about thirty miles away. (Stein 1986: 368) A map of the area also shows Auschwitz as about seventy-five miles away. After her time of nursing service, she started teaching in the school where she had grown up. (Stein 1986: 394) It was employment "which others could understand, one which you could discuss at the family table, whereas my studies had removed me into an inaccessible world." (Stein 1986: 394) While teaching full time, she nevertheless continued writing her dissertation. When she got home from school, she withdrew to write until the evening meal; right afterwards, she returned to her doctoral work. At ten o'clock at night, she would begin to prepare her classes for the next day. That summer, she lost twenty pounds. Her loss of appetite recurred nearly every year thereafter. She reflected:

> This led me to the realization that in the long run a combination of teaching with simultaneous, serious research was impossible. I saw clearly that, even though I really enjoyed it, I would abandon my teaching career without a moment's hesitation if I had the assurance that I was capable of producing a worthwhile scholarly work. For this reason Husserl's verdict on my dissertation was decisive for me in determining my life's direction.
>
> (Stein 1986: 396)

Husserl was also experiencing difficulty at this time. Stein later reports a heart to heart talk that Erika Gothe, a friend and colleague from Göttingen days, had with Husserl during the summer of 1916, when both women were in Freiburg:

> Erika had held a long conversation alone with the Master. He had complained about being unable to make any headway with his work. He had made an outline of the second part of his *Ideen zu einer Phänomenologie und phänomenologischen Philosophie* [*Ideas*] at the time he wrote the first part in 1912. After that first part had appeared in 1913, he had been pressed to give priority to getting out a new edition of the *Logische Untersuchungen* [*Logical Investigations*] since the old edition was out of print. Then had come the outbreak of the war, the death of his son Wolfgang, and the move to Freiburg. All of this had torn him from concentration on his work, and he had trouble finding his way back. He was unable to decipher the outline he had then written in pencil and in tiny shorthand; his vision was no longer good enough. He had been complaining for a long while about the weakness of his eyes, and he would have liked to have an operation for cataracts; but the condition would not ripen enough for surgery. Now there was but one resort left; he would have to have an assistant.
>
> (Stein 1986: 409)

Stein had seen Husserl in late 1915, before the time Erika had that conversation with Husserl. During the Christmas season of 1915, Edith had made her way up the Hohen Weg in Göttingen to the Husserl home, with her manuscript in hand. Although it was not the Master's custom to listen to anyone for long, she hoped for some attention, and during the visit he asked her to read long portions to him. He was satisfied and gave suggestions. Encouraged, Stein later continued her work back at home in Breslau. The work was not complete, however, when she heard the news that Husserl had received and accepted a call to Freiburg-im-Breisgau to succeed Heinrich Rickert. Without hesitation, Husserl accepted "one of the most respected chairs in philosophy in all of Germany." (Stein 1986: 386) Freed from his embarrassing position as a nontenured faculty member in Göttingen, he and Malvine were delighted. But their joy was cut short. While preparing for the move to Freiburg, news of the death of their son Wolfgang arrived.

Stein completed her manuscript on empathy as an act of knowing and on the constitution of the human person. During the Easter vacation in 1916, she dictated it to two stenographers, who typed it on good white bond paper. It became so bulky that she had to divide it into three sections, each bound in a soft blue cover; "finally, all three were enclosed in a firm case made to order for that purpose." (Stein 1986: 398) She mailed it to Husserl, asking him to read it so she could come to Freiburg in July for the oral exam. But he replied that, although he was happy to receive her work, he would not have time to read it. He needed all his time for his first semester in Freiburg and the renewed effort in teaching it demanded. Stein nonetheless studied for the orals and prepared her clothes for the trip. She had never been to southern Germany.

On the way to Freiburg that summer, she met and rode in the train with Hans Lipps, a student from Göttingen days, who was returning from a furlough. He had recently visited the Master, and she asked if he knew if Husserl had read any of her thesis. Lipps replied:

> "Oh, he hasn't read a word! He *did* show it to me. Once in a while he unties the case, takes out the volumes, hefts them in his hand and says, with great complacency 'Take a look at the huge thesis Fräulein Stein has sent me!' Then, replacing them neatly in the case, he ties it up again."
> Laughing, I said, "Well, that's encouraging!"
>
> (Stein 1986: 399–400)

Lipps confessed to how inferior he felt in comparison to her, but the feeling proved to be mutual; in the past, she had found "such a depth of insight in his brief comments" that her work had seemed to her to be merely a dabbling. (Stein 1986: 400)

Stein recalled and described this conversation nineteen years later, in 1935. But here, her memoirs, begun at her mother's home in Breslau and taken along in October, 1933, to Cologne when Stein entered that Carmel, were interrupted. (Stein 1986: 461) For, in the spring of 1935, she made her First Profession of Vows as a nun in the Carmel of Cologne, and her religious superiors asked her to complete a major philosophical work. (Stein 1986: 400) Stein returned to recording her memories only in January, 1939, after Husserl had died on April 27, 1938, and within a week after she had been moved to the Carmel in Echt, Holland, in an attempt to avoid being seized by the Nazis. She wrote only fifteen more printed pages. They are very important. They describe her crowning point, during the summer of 1916, when Husserl heartily approved her dissertation, and both she and the Master saw her true philosophical merit. Before this point, she did not have "the assurance that I was capable of producing a worthwhile scholarly work." (Stein 1986: 396) Husserl's verdict on her dissertation was, along with her own self-recognition, indeed decisive for her in determining her life's direction.

In the last fifteen pages, Stein describes how she enjoyed her trip to Freiburg in July, 1916, stopping along the way, and then getting lodgings in a farmhouse near the mountains of the Black Forest, before setting out for the Husserls' home.

> They lived on Lorettostrasse at the foot of the Loretto mountain ... They did not own a house as they had in Göttingen but rented a roomy apartment. As soon as I was admitted to the vestibule, I caught sight through a large glass door of my dear Master seated at his desk in his study. I was sorry about that. In Göttingen he had been able to work upstairs, completely separated from the world. At times when he had been working under particularly heavy pressure, he had not come down even for the evening meal. And here he was, now, seated as it were in a glass house. I was taken to him at once.
>
> He rose to meet me and called out, jokingly: "Execution is at hand!"
>
> (Stein 1986: 402–3)

He still had not looked at her thesis. He invited her to attend the new course he was currently teaching: modern philosophy as seen from "the phenomenological attitude." But he could not give her the doctoral exam at this time. Frau Husserl, however, was appalled. "Fräulein Stein has made the long journey from Breslau to Freiburg especially for that purpose, and now it is all to be in vain!" (Stein 1986: 403) Husserl would not be moved. "Fräulein Stein is happy to get to know Freiburg and to see how I am settling in here. She will also gain a great deal from my course. She can get her doctorate next time." (Stein 1986: 403) Stein did not despair; she attended his course, four times a week, from five o'clock to six o'clock in the afternoon, with Frau Husserl. One day, the Master said:

> "Fräulein Stein, my wife gives me no peace! I am to take the time to read your work. So far, I have never accepted anyone's thesis before I was thoroughly familiar with it. But I will do so this time. Go to the Dean to make an appointment for the *Rigorosum*. But make the date as late as possible so that I can go over your thesis by that time."
>
> (Stein 1986: 404)

"*Rigorosum*" refers to rigorous examinations that, along with the writing of a dissertation, constitute the major requirement for a doctorate. Usually it is the job of a dissertation director in a university to challenge a graduate student thoroughly. I have never heard of a director giving approval before reading the student's draft and suggesting many revisions. Often the process is an ordeal. Husserl showed great confidence in Stein when he accepted her thesis before even beginning to read it. He relied on his earlier perception of her understanding and originality. In the end, she did not disappoint him.

Stein left him a carbon copy, handed in the original to the faculty office, and asked two other professors to be examiners. All was set for August 3, 1916. She attended several lectures by the other professors, but in the mornings she carried her books to a meadow and studied for the exams. Her friend from Göttingen, Erika Gothe, came to be with her—to study her thesis and accompany her to Husserl's lectures. While they did not miss any of Husserl's classes, they also took several mountain hikes and gazed at the Alps. One day at the railway station, they noticed the Husserl family on the platform, getting on another coach of the same train. "We got the impression that they were as reluctant to have us see them as we were to be seen by them," Stein recalls. (Stein 1986: 406) The Husserls' living son, Gerhart, was home on a short leave. Perhaps they did not want to pay attention to anyone else, even as the traveling Edith and Erika may not have wanted to appear unstudious.

Husserl was straining to do well in his new post. Stein was his first student to take a doctoral exam in Freiburg. He wanted her to make a good first impression. She regretted he was now living in a "glass house," subject to the scrutiny of others, having to try to look good. When Erika spoke to their professor alone (in the long conversation presented earlier as a quotation), she found he was burdened and sad: he could not make headway in *Ideas*, his son Wolfgang had died, he could not see well. Still, he was now spending much time studying Stein's thesis and was finding her "to be very independent." (Stein 1986: 408)

The evening after Erika had spoken with Husserl and heard about his difficulties, Stein listened to her report, back at their lodgings. They racked their brains until late.

> "If I thought I could be of any use to him," I said, finally, "I would come [to stay in Freiburg]." ... Neither had I any financial resources from which to support myself.... I would just simply do it. But what still seemed inconceivable to me was that he would even consider me. I was such a little thing, and Husserl was the first in rank of all the living philosophers. In fact, I was convinced he was one of those real giants who transcend their own time and who determine history. (An aside: I am writing this on April 27, 1939. One year ago today, the beloved Master entered eternity.) But there was a solution to the problem. "I'll ask him personally. But I can wait until the examination is over. When he has finished reading the dissertation, he will be in a better position to judge."
>
> With that we ended our discussion and said good-night.
>
> (Stein 1986: 410)

The following evening, after his lecture, Husserl came down the stairs and told his wife to go on ahead with Erika Gothe, as he had something he wanted to talk about with Edith Stein, who waited in suspense for what he might say. Just a few days before he had said: "Your thesis pleases me more and more. I have to be careful that my satisfaction with it doesn't get too exalted." (Stein 1986: 410) Now he continued his praise. He had gotten far in her work and found her to be really "a very gifted little girl." (Stein 1986: 410) Becoming more serious, he told her he was deliberating if her work could be put in the *Yearbook*, the first phenomenological journal, along with his *Ideas*. "I have an impression that in your work you forestall [anticipate, deal with in advance] some material that is in my second part of *Ideas* [the part he had outlined but not yet written in full]." (Stein 1986: 411) His *Ideas* were to be published in the first edition of the journal, and he was wondering if her work too could be included, as she had written in advance what he had only sketched. She was ahead of him in writing about empathy and the experience of another person as central to our knowing of the world.

Stein remembers:

> His words gave me a jolt! Surely this was the moment to ask him. Seize the opportunity by the scruff of the neck!
>
> "If that is really so, Professor, then there's a question I have been meaning to put to you. Fräulein Gothe told me of your need for an assistant. Do you think I might be able to help you?"
>
> At that point we were just crossing over the Dreisam. The Master stood stock still in the middle of the *Friedrichsbrücke* and exclaimed in delighted surprise: "You want to help me? Yes! With you, I would enjoy working!"
>
> I do not know which one of us was more elated. We were like a young couple at the moment of their betrothal. In the Lorettostrasse, Frau Husserl and Erika stood watching us.
>
> Husserl said to his wife: "Think of it! Fräulein Stein wants to come to be my assistant."
>
> Erika looked at me. We needed no exchange of words to reach an understanding. Her deep-set, dark eyes were alight with intense joy. That night when we went to bed she said, "Good night, Lady Assistant!"
>
> (Stein 1986: 411)

Stein would begin in October and receive 100 Marks per month. Beforehand she would have to study the Gabelsberger method of shorthand that Husserl used. On August 3, the Dean sat with his back to Stein and Husserl but listened attentively to the intimate exchange of views that her oral examination with the Master came to be. The two other examiners were impressed. Once, when Stein could not remember a name, Husserl prompted her. At the Husserls' later in the evening, Malvine and Elli, their daughter, had made a wreath of ivy and daisies, and they put it on her head in place of a laurel wreath. "Just like a queen!" said Rudolf Meyer, a young Protestant theologian in attendance. Husserl was "beaming with joy. The Dean himself had proposed I be given the mark *summa cum laude*." (Stein 1986: 414) Late that night she and her friends walked home in the darkness of a total blackout because of the danger of an air raid. She was still wearing the wreath. The landlady at the farmhouse said her picture ought to be taken like that, "while the glow of happiness is still there. Otherwise, you've always got such a serious look on your face." (Stein 1986: 414)

After these words, there are a few lines about the next morning: Stein sends home a telegram about the good news and sets out on her return trip. Then her memoirs end abruptly. In August, 1942, about three years and seven months after writing these last few pages, she was murdered by Nazis in Auschwitz.

In the last events recounted in her memoirs, Stein's self was apparent, the self that was the turning-point of her whole personality. Surely it was not her ego who was briefly crowned a queen. Through Husserl's help, Stein came to see the fundamental worth of the power constituting her, although she probably knew this power much more in January, 1939, while completing her recollection of events, than she had understood herself in 1916. Nevertheless, Husserl was a likeness to her own "animus," Jung's term for masculine spirit and strength in a woman. Thus, she was not wholly dependent upon Husserl for knowing herself, as her own spirit by its trials and challenges was awakening and enabling her to know herself and her life's direction—that long way upon which she had been travelling since she first had gone to Göttingen and which had now recently brought her to Echt. Remembering in detail the main events of her life years afterwards, and feeling their significance in new ways, gave Stein access to a deeper level of her subjectivity, as well as a clearer sense of a relationship that brought her into, as Jung says, "absolute, binding, and indissoluble communion with the world at large." (Jung 1966: 178) Although in community with her Carmelite sisters, she nevertheless remained bound to her wider Jewish family, and was to suffer death with them.

Despite the great joy and promise Stein and Husserl had felt while crossing over the Dreisam, "like a young couple at the moment of their betrothal," they were not able to collaborate, even though Stein continued her work as his assistant for a year and a half. She wrote about the difficulty to Roman Ingarden, an old friend from their Göttingen days who was part of the celebration when she wore the wreath of ivy and daisies, and said that Husserl's "thoughts have become frozen." (Stein 1993: 12) She also told Ingarden: "we hardly talk together anymore" (Stein 1993: 6) and "the Master tires so easily and is so slow," (Stein 1993: 16) and she was "certain that, left alone, the Master simply would not publish anything more. I consider the publication of his work more important than any possible products I might eventually present to the world." (Stein 1993: 16) For this reason, she undertook the editing necessary for publication: she read his shorthand, organized his papers, and transcribed the pages by hand, filling in what he had outlined. But afterwards, he did not read the results of her efforts.

Stein wrote to Ingarden:

I have a burning desire for a thorough discussion with the Master about the work I have accomplished so far before I take up something else. I simply have no will at all to amass a new stack of papers he won't even look at.

(Stein 1993: 13)

Erika Gothe visited Stein in the spring, 1917, and read Stein's edited draft of Husserl's *Ideas* so Stein could at least discuss her work with someone. But Stein's hope—"If only the Master could finally be brought to read them over!"— remained unfulfilled. (Stein 1993: 14) Moreover, he had not made a critical appraisal of her thesis on empathy. Stein was especially grateful to Ingarden for giving her his review of it, as the first appraisal she had received. But even when her thesis was published, she complained that she "never had as much as a comment on it from the Master himself." (Stein 1993: 15) She was young then, and was still depending more on the outer appearance of masculine spirit in a man than she was recognizing the immanent appearing of her own animus, her own masculine spirit, as a means of knowing and valuing herself in the deepest way.

Stein nevertheless continued to have a good relationship with Husserl. In 1926, two years before the Master retired, she visited him in Freiburg. It had been four years since her baptism on January 1, 1922; she had not seen him since she had ceased being his assistant eight years earlier, in 1918. She was able to be totally frank without trying to convert him to Catholicism. (Stein 1993: 60) In January, 1931, Stein was received most peaceably at the Husserl home. After dinner "the old folks" had "their afternoon nap – I, too, was made to lie down on a sofa – and then we could talk at leisure for a while longer. Frau Husserl took me to the train." (Stein 1993: 84)

Perhaps the most fortunate aspect of Stein's assistantship was her discovery that, during his years at Göttingen, Husserl had written about time on odd sizes of scraps of paper; as each was filled, it had been placed to a side in random order on his desk (in graduate school, I heard authoritatively that this placement of papers was Husserl's regular practice—"so that the ink could dry," we were told). These papers "were packed into haphazard bundles and were collected over the years with an expectation of their being put in order eventually." (Stein 1986: 416) After Stein finished the draft for the revision of *Ideas*, she turned her attention to these paper scraps. They inspired her and gave her some taste for continued work on Husserl's manuscripts, as she wrote to Roman Ingarden in July, 1917:

Recently I have been putting more and more stacks of manuscripts in order; I have just come upon the bundle on *Zeitbewusstsein* [time-consciousness]. You know best how important these matters are .... What I have is rather a sorry mess: scraps of paper from as far back as 1903. Still I am very eager to see whether it can be made into some kind of monograph. After all, that would represent a step toward print-readiness, even though there is no knowing whether and when publication will follow.... Now it seems to me, once more, that what I am doing here is not entirely without sense.

(Stein 1993: 18)

In 1928, the papers on time-consciousness were published; the last three lines of the foreword indicated that Fräulein Stein had inserted some chapter and paragraph divisions in her "stenographic transcription" in accord with some "marginal notes" of Husserl's. (Husserl 1964: 16) But she received no credit for understanding the significance of the work as a whole, putting the paper scraps in order according to her understanding of them, transcribing them all into grammatically correct sentences, and making these into a monograph ready for publication. In the end, she did not mind, as her main goal was "the publication of his work" as "more important than any possible products I might eventually present to the world." (Stein 1993:16) Nevertheless, I am not alone in owing her a great debt of gratitude. For over forty years, the meaning expressed in those "scraps of paper" that she made into a book has been on my mind, drawing me again and again to greater notice of the phenomena of awareness. Then, too, there is the personal influence she has had on me over the years, both as a woman philosopher and as a victim of the Shoah, the central spiritual event of the twentieth century, as Elie Wiesel spoke of it, saying: "But when I want to write about what is the most important Event of this century I cannot." (Wiesel 1995: 4) Stein is a model for empathy and honesty, and so in remembering her I am emboldened to include a letter I wrote to her years ago when I was first reading her writings; the letters I refer back to are in Stein (1993).

Dear Edith Stein,
This is Cecile Tougas, writing to you. I am grieved to learn that you and Husserl—after your moment of great hope and joy as you were crossing the bridge over the Dreisam, when "the Master stood stock still in the middle of the *Friedrichsbrücke*" and you "were like a young couple at the moment of their betrothal"—oh, that you were nonetheless unable to collaborate. You tried for a year and a half, but were disappointed.

  Dear woman philosopher, you did anticipate just what he was trying to write as *Ideas II*. You knew directly by empathy what he was having such difficulty coming to: a clear sense of the ways in which the feelings of one person are given in another's experience. He lived primarily in the flux of his thoughts, impressions, and distinctions, describing them faithfully and carefully on all those sheets of paper, so he could come to understand the flux better, but not primarily to teach someone else. From his own thoughts he had to reflect seriously in order to know the emotional life of others. He found empathy to be a puzzle he could not grasp immediately and directly, as you could. "The constitution of the other" was a problem for him. He had neither your gift, nor your habit of noticing another's meaning as it may be given in a glance—evident, for example, when you looked at Erika after you had just crossed the Dreisam with the Master: "Erika looked at me. We needed no exchange of words to reach an understanding. Her deep-set, dark eyes were alight with intense joy."

  When you sensed his inadequacy in perceiving and judging by feeling, you hit his sorest spot, and as you say in a letter, "his thoughts have become frozen."

(I am quoting from your letters to Roman Ingarden, your old friend from your Göttingen days, who was part of the celebration that night at the Husserls' when you wore the wreath of ivy and daisies: letter #10, p. 12.) Husserl did not know what to do, and your tacit confrontation, kind as your presence was, embarrassed him. Yet you had a powerful effect on him that became manifest only many years later. During the last decade of his life, when he was no longer a faculty member, he wrote a big work and a number of smaller lectures that had the term "the crisis" in their titles: then his feeling for others and for Europe's growing sickness overflowed into words.

Meanwhile, those years in Freiburg were a "dark night of the soul" for him (to use a phrase of your friend, Saint John of the Cross), just as they were depressing for you. His son had died, he could not see his writing, he was now living in a professional glass house. To the extent he recognized inadequacy in his former work, he could not make changes until he had new evidence. But he was dry and empty. He must have had some foreboding of what was to come for the Jews; the shadow of his final illness and death was slowly approaching. He was suffering the irony of at last having attained a good faculty position and decent academic notice—people were coming from the United States and even Japan to study with him—but the status did not fill the void in his life.

Every day he tried: he kept to his routine, the time at his desk and the time on his walk. But his feeling was a deep lake far inside and its waters were not reaching the surface. Above its flow was a thick crust of rigid words and phrases, awkward sentences and wandering paragraphs, through which he habitually expressed himself. His feeling was hardly making it into the world. How could a distinguished university professor, accustomed to academic language and hardened into professional formality, be himself openly? Husserl would then have had to reveal publicly that you—a woman thirty-four years younger than he was—knew about empathy and personality, and were writing lucidly about them, in ways he was barely groping for. Professors did not usually admit to such vast ignorance, and rarely do they do so now. Even if Husserl had been willing to accept humiliation, there was little social support for a man to be emotionally honest. There were few accepted models for a married man to talk to a young woman he was vehemently attracted to, without being unfaithful to his wife, or taking advantage of the young woman. How could he learn from you what he was desperately needing to know? What could crack open the thick crust over the dark lake of his feeling?

Years of pain made Husserl more receptive. When, as a retired professor, he was banned from the University campus because of his Jewish ancestry, the grief of one who had given a son to Germany rose and flowed forth, and he wrote from this flood about the crisis in Europe. But during the time he was wanting to collaborate with you, he was deeply in the dark night. At least he did not "fake it" with you by pretending to be clever. Nor did he try to seduce you—not that you wanted him to. He respected you, but he withdrew, frozen.

You wrote: "we hardly talk together anymore" (#5, p. 6) and "the Master tires so easily and is so slow" (#13, p. 16), and you are "certain that, left alone, the

Master simply would not publish anything more." (#13, p. 16) A parched man met your blooming youth, your frank questioning, your energetic desire to make his work accessible to others who would benefit from it as you had. While your vitality, beauty, and openness were just what he was lacking, he did not know what to do when faced with their power. He went on and bore the duties of each day.

How hard it must have been for you, who had hoped to work out directly with him your insights on the constitution of the human person! Instead, you had the drudgery of editing—facing a mess of papers, reading their difficult shorthand, organizing them into some coherent whole acceptable to readers, then transcribing the pages by hand, checking spelling and grammar and punctuation as you went along—tedious work. Afterwards, he did not even read the results of your efforts. You write to Ingarden: "I have a burning desire for a thorough discussion with the Master about the work I have accomplished so far before I take up something else. I simply have no will at all to amass a new stack of papers he won't even look at." (#11, p. 13) I am glad to learn that Erika Gothe visited you in the spring and read your draft of *Ideas* so you could at least discuss it with someone. What a disaster you report: "If only the Master could finally be brought to read them over!" (#12, p. 14) Moreover, I am saddened and angry to hear that he never made a critical appraisal of your thesis. When it was published, you "never had as much as a comment on it from the Master himself." (#13, p. 15) You did not deserve the neglect you suffered.

With regard to his own pressing task, the revision of *Ideas* in preparation for a second publication, Husserl had invited you to work on your own; he found himself unable to revise. He had an outline he could not read. You wrote to Ingarden: "I am now seeking to establish from the material at hand a unified draft of the entire thought process (of which I have a pretty clear view even though nothing is fixed or even carried to a conclusion)." (#6, p. 8) You hoped your draft would become the basis for the Master's work in getting the second, revised edition of *Ideas* published. Yet he did not collaborate, and the text you alone improved was published in 1922, without any credit being given to you for doing the work. (#5, p. 7, note 1) You wished he had just looked at the text, but never complained your name was not on it. What mattered to you was the accessibility of his thought to other people. You were a kind mediator between him and the world. Why did he not learn more from you?

It is March 12, 2001, many years after the Master's death and yours. Yet your lives affect mine so much that I feel you can hear me in some way. So, as it pours rain outside while it is dark and quiet inside, I who used to pray to statues of the Blessed Mother and Sainte Thérèse de l'Enfant Jésus (not Saint Teresa of Avila, from whom you are named Teresa Benedicta a Cruce) am writing to you, for today I cannot write about Husserl and you in any other way. Thank you for the strange manner in which you are present.

Unworthy (this was your word),
Cécile Thérèse

P. S. It is January 20, 2002. In some way, you are right behind me, dressed in a Carmelite habit, with your left arm on my left shoulder. I am writing without my glasses because of the tears. You went to your death in this clothing, but it does not smell bad. You are kind to me today, and glad I am still writing about you and Husserl. The crust of rigid words and phrases is so hard in academic life. Oh yes, break through, you say, with a sad smile I cannot see but do feel. You deign to visit me as I am having a hard time telling what is most important. There are several beautiful birds on the little tree just outside. A reddish one stays. You are still behind me. You were grievously neglected, mistreated, killed, yet you come forward to support me. Thank you very much.

# Chapter 13

# Expectation and its double intentionality

Expectation is a mode of intentional activity by which phenomena of a certain kind are present: appearances of what is not yet present, but is, rather, about to be. This description may sound strange at first, but let us see what happens as we try to pay attention to appearances that are not yet here, but are merely expected.

Awareness of something given as expected is primary and fundamental to all intentional life, just as memory is. Expectation is a spontaneous tending toward an open continuity of successive duration. It is a dependence on possibility, on what might be, or could be, or ought to be. It is a desire aiming at fulfillment that is not yet here. It is an interest in the future as the about to be. It means the future in advance.

Anything that is present now used to be an about to be. It became present only in relation to an expecting intent, however vague or marginal that intent may have been, even as merely the open intent "that something will be present." What is becoming present also depends on a successive retention of expectation, so that when the expected arrives it is experienced as a fulfillment that is meaningful in relation to expectation. A seeking is not fulfilled without somehow being retained as a "just having been seeking." Presentation is a gradation of transition, a "continuous shading-off," in which expectation exists inseparably with attention and memory. (Husserl 1964: 70)

Expectation is, at the same time, a distinct mode of intentionality. It makes the about to be a vital if unknown part of the present moment. Just as memory retains the past as past, successively in each new moment, so expectation holds in advance the about to be as about to be, successively in each new moment. On the basis of this spontaneous intending, I can more or less deliberately, and more or less specifically, anticipate the future. I can make plans, hope for outcomes, prophesy through signs, and forecast the weather. I can thus have the future as partially and indirectly present, inasmuch as expecting is full of countless possibilities.

The might be, the should be, and the ought to be live in expectation. The freedom of expectation may even exceed the freedom of memory, even though memory may have the wealth of a lifetime. For the force of what could be exceeds the limit of what has been. Awesome yet potentially undermining, expectation can unsettle the present as well as revitalize it. Most of all, expectation allows the flexibility of fulfillment its due influence in living experience, thus loosening the confines of what is and what has been. It is, indeed, a necessary part of the expansion of attentive interest. Perhaps it is neglected for fear it would destroy what is present, even while enriching the present tremendously. Expectation is thus both a creative and a destructive force, driving at what can become and what ought to become, in relation to what can no longer be. It draws the ego towards still unlived aspects of self as the whole to which ego belongs.

Without the expansion of interest that expectation brings to attention, human experience is stunted. In an extreme case, life becomes blocked. A radio program made by adolescents in Maine shows how hope in future possibility is crucial. On the teen talk show "Blunt" on WMPG 90.9, radio station of the University of Southern Maine, Gorham-Portland, on January 16, 1995, several young people and two adults, invited as guests, discussed suicide and its prevention. Then a young woman named Rose phoned in and engaged the panel in what became for them an intense conversation. In a bored voice, Rose said that she did not want to live and had not wanted to live for a long time, ever since she could remember. At sixteen, nothing really interested her. She claimed that her family had treated her well and her schoolwork was decent, but that she could understand why a friend had recently wanted to kill himself. When he was finding no compelling purpose for living, she could not find any in herself to suggest to him. He subsequently ran away from home. She could not see herself living beyond twenty. She wanted to see a few places, and then she was finished with life.

The response of the radio panel to Rose was both controlled and emotional. What had started as a talk show explaining ways of suicide prevention had actually become an instance of trying to prevent suicide. The attention of panel members intensified as they kept Rose on the line and asked her very direct questions. Nothing interests you at all? Do your parents know how you feel? Do you have a plan to kill yourself? How do you think your friends will feel whey they learn you have killed yourself without your telling them in advance how you felt? Why not tell them, when you feel safe that they won't tell authorities? Later another caller explained how she had felt like Rose until she realized that she did not have to fulfill the expectations of others by going to college; she could do "just about anything" after high school.

Rose makes it evident that one's own expectation is an essential part of vital energy. Without the original individual emergence of expectation, as distinct from the forced expectations of others, continuing seems impossible. In order to endure, attention depends on a strong tending toward future possibility. Even though a future fulfillment is not yet here, the absence of fulfillment is not the killer that the failure to expect is. The utmost presence of expectant energy is a love "that hopes all things" as spoken of in St. Paul's first letter to the Corinthians (13: 7). But the utter denial of expectant energy is a despair that strangles life. Through imagining a Chinese fairy tale about the ghost of a hanged woman, as this tale was studied in a university class, a double intentionality in expectation becomes manifest. For there is a mutuality, a reciprocal relation of whole self and ego as a part of self, in expectation, that strengthens hope and carries life forward. Both the possibility and the actuality of this reciprocal relation can become strikingly evident in imagining the tale, "The Ghost of the Hanged Woman" from *Chinesische Volksmärchen* as recounted by Marie-Louise von Franz. (Von Franz 1983: 135–7)

This Chinese story begins by differentiating the ghosts of people who hang themselves as the worst type of ghost. Generally, these are ghosts of poor peasant women who committed suicide because they were ill-treated, hungry, or overworked, and unable to see their way out of trouble. This type of ghost is so bad because she continually tries to seduce other women into hanging themselves, in hopes of finding a substitute for herself and returning to life.

The story then focuses on a soldier traveling to the capital who has to stay overnight in a poor village where the only shelter is an old temple in ruins and dust. After he shuts his eyes, he feels a cool wind, and then notices a woman sneaking out of the temple. He pretends to be asleep but sees she has a cord up her sleeve. He thus knows that this is a ghost of a woman who committed suicide. Unnoticed, he follows her to the hut of a desperate peasant woman twenty years old. Through the window, he sees a young mother crying with her baby. And then he sees the ghost on the rafters, swinging the rope in front of the poor woman's face. Just as the young mother is about to hang herself, the soldier bangs on the window and breaks in shouting. The ghost disappears, but leaves the rope behind. The man grabs it "and then lectured the woman, telling her not to be so stupid, that she should rather look after her child and that she had only one life." (Von Franz 1972: 136–7) Having "only one life" means her life is unique, irreplaceable, and individual; no ghostly substitute can or should live it for her.

After rescuing the young woman, the soldier returns to the temple with the rope and meets the ghost on the way. He refuses to give her the rope and she is furious. She becomes monstrous and tries to grab him. In resisting her, the man hits his own nose and gets a nosebleed. His human blood repels her. Still she curses him, and all night he is flinging his fists and shouting. In the morning, grateful villagers find him thus animated, with the rope that had been wound around his arm now grown into his flesh and become a red ring. The sun rises and he leaves town.

When this fairy tale was presented to a university class, several students drew in color what they felt was the crucial scene. One student drew the ghost as she was becoming monstrous—with a vivid greenish-black face, wild tangled hair, bloodshot eyes, and tongue stuck far out. It was a horrible yet wonderful drawing. Another drew the soldier's arm with the red ring grown into it, and remarked that the soldier was now wedded—he had committed himself to saving a woman and a child, and now he saw his military service as existing for the sake of women and children. But the drawing I remember most vividly had the soldier framed in the window, just as the young mother was dressing in new clothes and making herself up, in preparation for hanging herself. The little cradle was below, and the ghost was on the rafter above. This drawing had carefully indicated many details of the scene. In fact, a police officer in the class remarked how real it was, and said he often found in his police work that many women attempting suicide were discovered beautifully dressed and carefully made up. What struck me was the soldier framed in the window. But the student then corrected me: "No, that is not the soldier in the window," he said. "That is the mirror, showing her reflection as she dresses and makes herself up."

I apologized and wondered how I could have taken a dressed up woman for a shouting soldier. On closer inspection, however, I saw that it was indeed the woman in the frame. But I had first seen the man, the rescuer, in what was drawn as her reflection. At that moment a powerful insight came to me: my first view had not been completely wrong. In the mirror was the woman, but so was the man. For in her reflection was the presence of her animus, her masculine spirit and strength, as he was coming to her attention, just before his animating energy brought her to her senses, affirmed the importance of her baby, and saved their lives. His persistent affirming and intelligent valuing of her "only one life" were just what she needed and just what he provided. He was in her own reflection just as she was in it. He enabled her to see herself as a whole. When she too affirmed her self through the vigor of his intent, she began to hope and her life could continue. In such reflection, there is a double seeing: the self as a whole sees the ego and the ego becomes aware of this fuller seeing.

In paying attention to the wider viewing of self, the young woman comes to see what might be, or could be, or ought to be. The latter are modes of being that are not concrete sensate things, any more than animus as masculine spirit is. But they are modes of being nonetheless, insofar as life cannot go on without them. Indeed, most of the baby's life is in the future, as the young mother begins to appreciate, now that she can turn her attention beyond the concrete into the not yet seen. Hope, by definition, is in things unseen. Any kind of expectation provides to the present moment a dimension of otherness in which the mutual intending of self as whole and ego as part can be glimpsed, affirmed, and acted on.

# Chapter 14

# Double intentionality in dreaming

In his lectures on internal time-consciousness, which Edith Stein prepared for publication, Husserl distinguished in paragraphs 16–17 two basic kinds of intentionality: the presentational and the not presentational (or representational). (Husserl 1964: 60–4) His prime example of presentational intentionality is sense perception as direct awareness of what is itself given as bodily and originally present, as itself there. Without being adequately or completely given, the perceived is partially present, but genuinely so, as itself. Thus, perception fulfills, at least partially, what bare tending toward meaning intends. Perception is an act that gives what it means. It necessarily involves the presence of whatever is meant, as originally there as meant.

Presentational intentionality is a tending toward whatever is "placed before" awareness in some way, as introduced or presented, according to the first two senses of the German word *Vorstellung* listed in the dictionary: "introduction, presentation (*at court, etc.*); performance, representation; complaint, remonstrance, expostulation; imagination, idea, notion, conception, mental image." (Betteridge 1958: 548) *Vorstellung* can thus also refer to the first performance of a play, to a complaint, or to anything anyone might have in mind. Its wide range of meaning includes both the presentation of something directly given and the representation of something not directly given.

Besides sense perception, another mode of presentational intentionality is empathy. According to Edith Stein in her dissertation, empathy is perception of the other as distinct from self. Empathy is the actual experience of another self, another consciousness as other, and so it is "a kind of act of perceiving *sui generis*." (Stein 1989: 11) It is a presentation of another's experience to someone who is, by definition, not having that experience firsthand. Although empathy does not give the other's experience in the same way in which it is originally given for that other, empathy is still presentation. For we do know how others feel, at least in limited and correctable ways; the feelings of others are present to us, even when we do not have the same feelings that they have at that moment. They are given as the experience of what first of all belongs to another. Empathy gives what sense perception alone cannot give: awareness of what another person is experiencing from a point of view that is different from that of the other.

Another kind of presentational intentionality is retention, which, as Husserl writes, is direct consciousness of the "*just-having-been* of the 'just past' in its self-givenness, in the mode of *being self-given*." (Husserl 1964: 61) Retention tends toward and gives originally, although inadequately, the presence of the just-past itself, as just past. It is the direct awareness of what has just been, as an inseparable part of any ongoing presenting. Indeed, sense perception and empathy cannot occur without it. Any example of presentation depends on retention, which Husserl calls "primary remembrance," insofar as presentation cannot endure successively without it.

There are still other kinds of presentational intending. Expectation makes the about to be a vital part of the present moment, insofar as what might be, should be, or ought to be do exist as possibilities. Expectation makes present the existence of possibilities as such, and the forceful reality of these is often overlooked.

In a broad sense, any act of intuiting is presentational. By the term "intuition," Husserl means a beholding of anything at all, according to the meaning of the Latin word *intueor*, "look at, watch; contemplate, consider; admire." (Kidd 1961: 179) We may intuit a number as present to our mathematical gaze; we may observe a logical relation as obviously evident; we may simply be contemplating the Equal. When any tending toward meaning is at least partially fulfilled by the presence of a corresponding kind of "thing," that intending is presentational. We may then notice that we live among a wide variety of things—feelings, hopes, numbers, ideals—that are not spatial objects but that do exist nonetheless as immensely significant for us. Moreover, many sensate objects, such as money, computers, calendars, and grades all depend upon the existence of non-sensate numbers and logic. A thing does not have to be concretely sensate in order for it to exist and exist powerfully.

Some intentional acts are not presentational. Representation is not an original intending insofar as its stretching out towards meaning is not fulfilled by the presence of the thing meant. Rather, to represent is to make "as if" present, to place something "before us in images, as it were (if not precisely in the manner of true figurative consciousness)," writes Husserl. (Husserl 1964: 63–4) Representation puts before us an image, symbol, or indicator of some sort that leads us beyond this given to what is given only indirectly and inadequately. When, for example, we recall and reproduce an event of the far past in a remembrance Husserl counted as secondary, or when we simply imagine a possibility, we have first of all reproductions or images; by means of these, we also have what is not directly present. When we represent a transfinite number, we directly have a concept that indirectly symbolizes the meaning belonging to the number that far exceeds what is present to us.

Indeed, most things that are before us as themselves are present to us incompletely, inadequately, and thus to some extent indirectly, as intuited in only a few of the possible ways in which they might be intuited. Through representational consciousness, we have a sense of these other ways in which they might be given. If we count all that is "co-present" in the margins, horizons, or fringes of direct consciousness, we have to conclude that much indeed is represented. For whatever is actually present is tied to what is "co-present" and involves it—for example, a backside perspective of a thing just before us, a view of the city from a roof not ascended to, the feelings of strangers, the distinct relations that 3 has to each of the other numbers. Reciprocally, representation necessarily depends upon the presence of something that is there, that reminds, points beyond, symbolizes. It is now clear that presentational intentionality and representational intentionality are distinct yet interdependent. Hence, the ambiguity of the meaning of the German word *Vorstellung* as both "presentation" and "representation" is fitting and important, as it reflects the interesting inseparability of direct presence and indirect presence in our experience.

Dreaming is an intentional act that is both presentational and representational. First of all, a dream is an experience that is lived, that we find ourselves subjected to. When we are in a dream, we rarely doubt our experience: what is given is present in its bodily reality, as itself. Only after we awaken do we notice we have been dreaming and so have a perspective on the dream that is distinct from the one lived in the dream.

Three days ago, I dreamed of a colleague who had died ten months ago. He was to my left in a light brown three-piece suit, talking happily and steadily. I look at him again. I look again and see he is there, truly there. He is smiling and bubbling over in words. Grinning, he is. I don't notice what he is saying. But he is at the time so much there. After I awaken, and after several days, I continue to think about the dream in which he is a presence to me. He was here. His death and the dream call attention to his having been here. I cannot remember a dream that is a stronger presentation of an existence than this one.

Dreaming is also a representational reality. It provides a scene and events that point to something else beyond them. It gives an image or symbol of what is not directly present. Last month, I dreamed I was with President Obama on a large airplane. He comes and sits in a row in front of me, a long row that does not have an aisle. I tell a few people that he is there. I think I will go tell him that I dreamed I met him (in fact, I had dreamed of him previously), but then I decide not to; after all, it is not that important. Later, we are going up two or three stairs in a place where he is to meet people, speak, and work. I feel really good to be with him. Reflecting on the dream later, I noticed that his presence too was strong. When I had dreamed of Obama previously, his wife and daughters were there, and it was an experience in which I felt I was meeting them personally also. Yet this dream is to me now a more representational dream than the dream of my colleague who had died. The dreamed meeting with Obama symbolizes mutual support and a joining of forces. I am a high school teacher and feel I am working towards a goal that he is working towards: the education of citizens in a democracy. The meeting strengthened my commitment to working with high school students and encouraged me to continue. My students and my teaching were not directly present in the dream, but they were indicated, suggested, and involved in the meaning of the situation. The tending energy of the dream as a whole affirmed their importance.

I have observed and recorded my dreams since 1982. Most dreams taught me, helped me, corrected me, or expressed something I was not able to express during the day. They have been a close friend to me, although I continue to feel that they are strange and that I do not know what they are. I live with them the way I lived with my cat for thirteen years; he was half wild and I was nearly always a bit afraid of him. But we had a wordless agreement: I would feed him and take care of his basic needs, and he would be my companion. He predeceased me, but dreams have such authority that I do not feel they will predecease me. Dreams are very close, closer than even a cat, a best friend, or a lover, but even in their teaching and their creating of me, they seem foreign and unknown. They show me aspects of myself that I would not otherwise know, and they draw me towards what I alone would not have thought. Dreaming seems to be a continual working on something that is not just one thing, or rather, that is a thing that is changing as it goes along. The authority of a dream is regal, like Queen Elizabeth II and at the same time like the Baba-Yaga in Russian fairytales, "the great Mother Nature .... the Great Goddess of Nature.... the Goddess of Death, which is an aspect of nature." (Von Franz 1983: 161) I realize I have long felt that dreaming is a reality that doesn't even think about going away, not being there, not existing. The double intentionality of presenting and representing in dreaming seems always to be putting aspects of reality before us in various interdependent ways.

# Intentional activity as the work of spirit

After 1933, Husserl could no longer speak publicly or publish his work in Germany. While he had many invitations to lecture in other places, including the University of Southern California, he stayed at his desk trying to complete his great final work, *The Crisis of European Sciences and Transcendental Phenomenology*, part of which was published in Belgrade in 1936. He did speak in Vienna and Prague, cities not far from his birthplace. In Vienna, he had lecture notes that he had spent many months preparing. Yet standing before the Cultural Society in Vienna on May 7, 1935, he left his notes unread and spoke freely for two and a half hours, making such a strong impression that he was asked to give the lecture again two days later. (Landgrebe 1980: 69) Afterwards, he continued working on it under the manuscript title, *The Crisis of European Humanity and Philosophy.* (Husserl 1977a: 5–10) The Prague lecture was incorporated into his great final, yet unfinished, work. (Husserl 1970a) By 1937, he was ill.

The young Jean Cavaillès, a brilliant logician, had attended Husserl's lectures at the Sorbonne in 1929, and described him as "very much the small town university type, in a frock coat and bespectacled, but in his delivery [were] the warmth and the simplicity of the true philosopher." (Spiegelberg 1965: 168) I imagine Husserl to be like this six years later in Vienna, but thinner, burdened, older, wearing the kind of thick glasses that people who had had cataracts used to wear at that time. Vienna was the city in which he had fallen in love with philosophy while listening to the lectures of Franz Brentano, the place he had returned to in visiting his old mother. He may have felt that this would be his last visit, and he must have been missing "the old European world." In his inaugural lecture upon coming to Freiburg in 1916, he "had understood World War I as the collapse of the old European world, in which spiritual culture, science, and philosophy had held an incontestable position." (Landgrebe 1980: 69)

Imagine May 7, 1935, at the Cultural Society in Vienna. Husserl stands up, an old professor, but as he speaks, there is growing passion. He is gripped by the importance of philosophy in a cultural life that needs renewal now more than ever before. The philosopher says: "*Unsere Umwelt ist ein geistiges Gebilde in uns und unserem historischen Leben. Le monde qui nous environne est une oeuvre de l'esprit, en nous et dans notre vie historique."* (Husserl 1977a: 24–5) This may be translated as: Our surrounding world is a work of spirit, in us and our historical life. The lived world is given us through mostly spontaneous intentional activity. How absurd it is, then, to pretend to be able to know this active spirit "objectively and materially" through natural science! Rather, we must first recognize that natural science itself is a spiritual, intentional work of scientists; then we can see how an objective, material, natural science is grossly inadequate to know subjectivity. We must therefore reflect on our experience directly as we are living it. Such reflective knowing is a genuinely philosophical task with infinite scope. It is also a task for humanity and will effect a renewal in cultural life. Without personal philosophical reflection, we are lost in "material nature."

Europe's sickness—now reaching a critical turning point, a crisis—consists in its mistaken rationalism, its naïve "objectivism" according to which spiritual, intentional life is presumed to exist in nature as a quality of natural, physical objects. This attitude of "naturalism" implies that spirit is a real part of real objectivity, is produced by physical causality, and exists spatially with everything else. But presuming that "all is material, objective nature" is an absurdity: observe your awareness, your perceiving at this moment, and notice that the aspects of real things you are perceiving are lived aspects, appearing in a flow with a horizon. How can this intentional flow—of perceptions, hopes, dreams, agonies—that we are observing (even as we are subjected to it) be thought to be reducible to some real, physical, spatial thing? It is not even reducible to me or to you as a deliberate agent.

While an erroneous rationalism has not prevented scientists from achieving technological wonders, it has nonetheless kept them from important self-knowledge. Something is distressingly wrong: in their work, objectivist scientists naïvely presuppose rational norms and methods of scientific knowing, yet they cannot account for the authority of these ideals they depend upon. How indeed can any authoritative norm, universal method, or necessary ideal exist as part of their work? For if, overlooking their own perceptual field, they assume that intentional life is a real part of real objectivity, and that spirit is produced by physical, spatial causality, they have no way of accounting for the existence of any authoritative nonmaterial ideal—even the ideals and norms they are guided by and depend on in their work. These, among positivists, acquire the status of "merely posited assumptions," or, among pragmatists, they are "useful fictions."

Yet, in everyday life, we feel the powerful existence of ideals and norms that no one has ever seen realized—indeed, we live by nonmaterial numbers, "impossible" goals, and wild hopes as urgently valid. These do not exist anywhere in space. Old Europe had esteemed them as worthy of unending philosophical reflection and dedicated aspiration. What a crushing blow to have to deny them all, in order to participate in an increasingly scientific "rational" age!

Members of the Cultural Society in Vienna stand up in tears and applaud vehemently for a long time; I imagine them glad to feel a moment's relief from the rigid, narrow, totalitarian attitudes threatening them as personal subjects of living intending. Like the members of the Cultural Society, Husserl struggled not to be suffocated but rather to find spirit as living breath and air. During his last years, he suffered from pleurisy, an inflammation of the membrane surrounding the lungs. He could not live in materialism. What is a materialist? In running the death camps, the National Socialists who saved bones for ashtrays and ground up burned bodies to provide calcium for agricultural fields were materialists: they felt they were not wasting anything.

If Husserl could speak before us all today for one minute, I imagine he would say: "Look at the ways in which things are given. Listen to a tone sounding. Look at an appearing house: the flowing appearances are not one meter away from the house 'in a brain,' but are, rather, non-independent from the house, even as they are non-independent from subjective experiencing. Appearances of the world are inseparable from subjectivity even as they are inseparable from the world, while appearances, world, and subjectivity are nonetheless distinct from one another. Notice their interdependence and distinction repeatedly. You will see then that 'transcendental subjectivity' refers to fundamental intentional accomplishments continually occurring in the formative temporal flux of experience. Notice the ongoing intentional activity of perceiving, thinking, remembering, feeling, expecting, imagining—even dreaming—in which, and through which, the presence of ourselves and the world is given. Observe whatever is given, in the varied ways there are of being given, within the limits of its being given, and accept it as genuine existence, in the widest sense of 'existence,' for numbers, ideals, and essences also exist and are inseparable from the communal life of spirit."

Not long before he died, Husserl wrote:

> Is it not paradoxical that no traditional psychology up to the present day has been able to give even a true exposition of perception, or even of the special type, the perception of bodies, or of memory, of expectation, of "empathy," or of any other manner of presentification [representation] .... Is it not paradoxical that no one had any idea of the diverse and difficult working problems contained under each of these headings?
>
> (Husserl 1970a: 249)

In his last weeks of writing, Husserl lamented the inadequacy of psychology. He found it paradoxical and troubling that psychologists—"students of the mind or soul"—seemed to have little or no sense of intentional activity as living and present for observation and description. So he recommended that they study sense perception, memory, expectation, empathy—intentional acts themselves as they are being lived. Noticing ways in which things are given was, he affirmed, a necessary introduction to the "difficult working problems" of psychology. He called for our repeated turning of attention toward the flow of experiencing so that we might come to have an explicit awareness of the non-independence of subjectivity and world. For he saw that our surrounding world is a work of spirit, in us and our historical life.

An editorial reader wondered about the relation between the phenomenology of Husserl and the work of Robert Stolorow, George Atwood, and Bernard Brandchaft who practice and write about "the intersubjective perspective" (1979, 1994, and 1995) as they seek to bridge different psychological theories and overcome a "subject–object" split that they find to persist in modern Western thought.

If we repeatedly study the subjective flux, however, we can see what Husserl meant when he wrote in *Logical Investigations, Volume Two*: "Where it makes nonsense to speak of isolation, the problem of overcoming such isolation is likewise nonsensical." (Husserl 1970c: 477) From the beginning, subjects are not split from one another, nor are objects split from subjects, insofar as we are primally given as non-independent of one another and non-independent of the other objects that are present to us in a variety of ways. Awareness is a continuum in which we participate as subjects to whom objects in the widest sense of the term are given. Studying a transfinite series, or trying to, is a way of coming to recognize the continuum of interdependent parts, each of which differs in some way from the rest. When psychologists begin with a study of awareness as a continuum, they do not need a bridge later on.

In regard to "the intersubjective perspective," Husserl would notice a problem with each of the words in the phrase. "The" with a singular noun means "one and only one." But in using the phrase, the authors seem to be referring to many perspectives occurring among several subjects, not just one perspective. Thus, the word "the" is misleading.

Then there is a problem with the word "intersubjective." The prefix "inter" means "between," and so the question may be asked, what is it that is between the subjects? In *The Intersubjective Perspective* (Stolorow 1994) there are many words referring to what is between: "boundary" (6); "field, worlds, contexts" (x and 28); "interface" (7); "point of intersection" (8), to give just a few examples. Yet these are spatial expressions used to try to speak about what is not spatial: the temporal flow of phenomena present for subjective awareness. Time is not identical to space. The temporal flux can be noticed and described in its own terms as it is being lived, as successive and enduring. Moreover, intentional activities can be examined and described as lived subjectively and individually in time, even as they are done together with another or with others. But succession and duration of moments and intentional activities do not exist in space, never mind in a space "in between" subjects. Mutual intentionality is not a matter of in and out, of internality and externality.

A perspective is a "seeing-through," and is a viewpoint of a subject. It is surely not a view from nowhere. It may indeed be a view of things and people in space. But a lived perspective of spatial objects, while inseparable from the objects, is not given as itself being in space, as the objects are. For a perspective belongs to the flux of an experiencing subject. It is meaningless apart from a subject who is "seeing through" that viewpoint. It does not exist between subjects, nor is there only one.

A mutuality of intentionality among individual subjects of awareness is given as non-independent of experience. If, however, we speak of "the intersubjective perspective," we are close to thoughtlessly presuming that there exists a point of view that is "out there between us," existing as separable from a subject seeing through it. While the perspective of an individual may indeed be changing from moment to moment, there is no perspective without a subject and no two people have an identical perspective. So "the intersubjective perspective" sounds like an object that is split away from any particular subject. But the split was the problem that was supposed to be fixed in the first place.

The editorial reader also asked for a comment about Irwin Z. Hoffman, author of *Ritual and Spontaneity in the Psychoanalytic Process: A Dialectical-Constructivist View* (1998), who holds as true that, across cultures and history, we humans collectively create meaning and construct what is present, that the principle of uncertainty holds, and that we are constantly threatened with nonbeing and nothingness. In response, calling upon Socrates and Kierkegaard, I would try to engage such a constructivist in a dialectical conversation by asking him to create a number that is not already there, or to put a very small fraction out of existence. If that did not show him that there is some meaning we are not able to create or destroy, I would ask him to create the meaning that we do not create meaning but rather are given meaning through undergoing experience over time. I would hope he would have a genuine experience of being given meaning.

Proceeding to the principle of uncertainty, I could ask whether the principle itself is uncertain or certain. For if the principle itself is uncertain, then maybe something is certain after all. Or if the principle itself is certain, then something is certain after all, namely, the principle. In doing this activity, the constructivist might become distracted from his presuppositions and, grieving their loss, might begin to notice his hunger for the infinite.

I would want Kierkegaard to show up in words and hold the constructivist close to the fire, in ironic logic and deep pathos, because that great Danish philosopher was anxious about an existing human subject in relation to the infinite. Kierkegaard said that a man who knows the truth objectively, but is not affected by it subjectively, is a madman one dare not look at "from fear of discovering that he has eyes of glass and hair made from carpet-rags; that he is, in short, an artificial product." (Kierkegaard 1941a: 175)

Husserl was no constructivist. Long after his death, in one year of the 1980s, the Simon Silverman Phenomenology Center at Duquesne University in Pittsburgh advertised a symposium on Husserl. Inside the notice was a brief story. Husserl had been asked what the most important problem in philosophy was, and he had replied, "Why, the problem of God, of course."

In the six or eight main works, depending on whether "main" means "large" or "important," published during his lifetime, however, Husserl rarely mentions the word "God." He refers to the way in which Descartes or some other modern philosopher thinks of God as a supreme rational principle, but does not write about how God matters to him. Husserl seemed not to be ready to address publicly this most important issue. He spent his life studying and writing about the phenomena of awareness. His years were filled with detailed examination of intentional acts and the careful making of distinctions. In this labor, his goal was to first provide a solid foundation for philosophizing. Late in life, he did not feel that he had done so, inasmuch as he did not stop trying to provide it. He did not desist from the process of purification.

Speaking of himself in the third person, Husserl wrote: "If he has been obliged, on practical grounds, to lower the ideal of the philosopher to that of a downright beginner, he has at least in his old age reached for himself the complete certainty that he should thus call himself a beginner." (Husserl 1958: 28) Dealing with great questions of God, life, and death, in a definitive philosophical way, was quite beyond one who had only begun the groundwork. And yet, his work shows infinite passion, as do his words that I have remembered by heart for forty years: "*Philosophie war die Mission meines Lebens. Ich* musste *philosophieren, sonst konnte ich in dieser Welt nicht leben.*" (Philosophy was the mission of my life. I *had to* philosophize; otherwise, I was not able to live in this world.) (Husserl 1968: 161, emphasis in original) Forty years ago, I heard these words repeated in graduate school, but did not note their exact source. Today, I discovered that they are written in a book of Husserl's letters to Roman Ingarden, a member of the Göttingen Circle and an old friend of Edith Stein; Ingarden was part of her doctoral celebration when she wore the wreath of ivy and daisies, and they too corresponded by letter. In his book of letters from Husserl, Ingarden included his own commentary and memories.

The occasion on which these words were spoken was the celebration of Husserl's seventieth birthday, April 8, 1929. Ingarden had been invited by Frau Professor Husserl but it appeared that he would not be getting his passport on time, so he wrote a letter of congratulations to Husserl with great regrets. But the next day the travel document did arrive, and so he hastened and arrived in Freiburg on the day of the celebration, early in the morning. At the hotel, he saw many old friends and went with them on time to the Husserl home on Lorettostrasse. Among his old friends were Edith Stein, Jean Hering, and Alexandre Koyré.

The official feast began as the Rector and the Dean showed up with Martin Heidegger, who, as new Ordinarius professor, also spoke and gave a long, rather complicated speech. Ingarden notes that, after two nights on the train, he was still not rested and so did not understand much of the speech. At the end, Husserl answered, visibly pleased, but unpretentious and brief. He agreed that much was given to him to complete, but much still lay unfulfilled. Then he closed with remarkable words. He said there was one thing he must reject, and that was the speech about merit. "*Ich habe gar kein Verdienst.*" (I have hardly merited anything.) "Philosophy was the mission of my life. I *had to* philosophize; otherwise, I was not able to live in this world." (Husserl 1968: 161, emphasis in orginal German) Ingarden says that these words gave him much to think about then and often afterwards; he was not the only one to be affected.

Living "in this world" was an issue that critics raised against Husserl's "transcendental idealism," the philosophical affirmation that experienced reality is fundamentally a work of spirit through mostly spontaneous intentional activity. Over a long period of time, Husserl observed that the world was not independent of its ways of being given to awareness, and he later wrote about the relation of world and givenness to subjectivity as "the universal a priori of correlation" whose breakthrough affected his life-work. (Husserl 1970a: 166n)

Yet critics misunderstood how the appearing world is an intentional accomplishment of spirit; perhaps, instead of understanding properly, they were imagining that "intentional accomplishment" referred to a solitary thinker constructing a fantasy world. I wonder, though, how they could have understood without being reminded of some basic mathematical insights. They did not recognize, or were not shown, that limit, transfinite number, and equivalence of two infinite series are crucial to grasping the essence of awareness in a beginning way. Without such preparation, it is very difficult to understand how a present moment as a limit holds an infinite series of infinite series, or how the phases of time-consciousness, as distinct yet inseparable, form a transfinite whole that continually exceeds itself. Without a sense of whole as continuum, the relation of subjectivity and objectivity is not understood as continuous, and so the relation is thought to be an insurmountable split because it concerns distinct things. Then subjectivity is assumed to be an object in the natural world, a real part of real objectivity; awareness is posited as being a characteristic of spatial things, like their color and their extension. Camus made such assumptions and consequently cried out that memory was buried in sand by wind, as I noted in Chapter 6.

Husserl seemed not to recognize the importance of teaching his audience some basic mathematical concepts that he knew well. His own understanding was growing; that task was hard enough without having to figure out how best to teach others what he was coming to understand. And so he was mistakenly identified with the idealist camp in the realist–idealist battle of modern Western philosophy, even though he had long since gone beyond that battle. Because of his great interest in subjectivity, he was accused of trying to escape from the world by means of "transcendental idealism." But philosophy was the way he lived in the world. He *had to* philosophize. On his seventieth birthday, he recognized that much still remained to be done. He had been right to feel certain that "he should thus call himself a beginner." (Husserl 1958: 28)

In repeated reflection, Husserl was pursuing awareness as live perceiving, remembering, and expecting, as that vital, intelligent, passionate spark of acting and suffering, that feeling and bearing of the weight of meaning: consciousness in all its varied forms in which the world appears, and through which the world is what it is. The flow of time, he recognized, is no mechanical process, no impersonal being, but rather a valuable experiencing in a spontaneous intending that also intends the essential form of "new now retaining past moments and anticipating future moments." Subjectivity is inescapable: Husserl could not escape its actuality and did not want to. He *had to* study phenomena of awareness in order to live in the world, for subjects and world are inseparable.

# Chapter 16

# Nebulous knowing

There are ways of perceiving and knowing that are difficult to describe. Jung uses the word "intuition" to name an intentional activity that is difficult not only to describe, but also to distinguish. In defining "intuition," Jung begins by giving its Latin root: "(L. *intueri*, 'to look at or into')." (Jung 1976b: 453) He knows, as Husserl does, that the term as used generally refers to any kind of observing awareness in which something is given as present in some way. But Jung uses the term most of the time in a special sense to mean something in particular that is "neither sense perception, nor feeling, nor intellectual inference, although it may also appear in these forms." (Jung 1976b: 453) The distinctive characteristic of intuition is that a "content presents itself whole and complete, without our being able to explain or discover how this content came into existence." (Jung 1976b: 453) It is an "instinctive apprehension" (Jung 1976b: 453) of something as given with certainty and conviction, but the source of the certainty and conviction is not apparent.

In sense perception, we do not know how perceptual phenomena come about, but we ground them in a sensate objectivity that others too can perceive. Intuition does not seem to have such a ground. It looks like prejudice, which is certainty without a basis. Moreover, Jung says that intuition is "characteristic of infantile and primitive psychology." (Jung 1976b: 454) Yet it happens and its gives aspects of reality, sometimes crucially important ones, which are confirmed only some time after the intuitive activity has occurred.

In revising my writing about Jung and his sense of "intentionality" in relation to Freud and Schopenhauer, I experienced an instance of seeming to have known something without knowing how I knew it. I heard a few words from someone. Almost at the same time, I read about an experience of the same specific content I had heard about, as being shared by Jung and a patient, as reported by a psychologist reading about Jung, and as subsequently mentioned in two newspaper articles. The appearance of this particular content to me, to Jung and a patient of his, to a psychologist reading about Jung, and in two newspapers seen by the psychologist, was strange. In the following pages I will say more about this odd coincidence.

Just before a renewed attempt at writing about Jung, Freud, and Schopenhauer, I found I was quite interested in reading an article in *The Economist* about the

*Hubble* space telescope orbiting Earth. This telescope in a space station has taken more than half a million photos over several years. In May, 2009, a mission to *Hubble* via the space shuttle had as one goal to "install a wide-field camera that will let the telescope see galaxies previously beyond its reach" so that astronomers "will be able to observe young, hot stars that glow mainly in the ultraviolet part of the spectrum," as well as "the first stars and galaxies that formed in the universe, which are now so old and distant that their light has been relegated to the infra-red part of the spectrum ...." (*The Economist* May 16, 2009: 85)

The article went on to report that, in the same month, the European Space Agency launched a satellite, *Planck*, to gather data on "the cosmic microwave background" which shows what happened only 380,000 years after the Big Bang, the moment "when matter started to coalesce and the universe became transparent." (*The Economist* May 16, 2009: 85) Small variations in the intensity of radiation of the microwave background show "the origins of what went on to become galaxies, stars, planets and, in at least one instance, intelligent life." (*The Economist* May 16, 2009: 85)

The thought of the first stars and galaxies that formed in the universe so long ago was dazzling to me, although I wondered what the Big Bang was, how it was given in experience, and what kind of awareness was noticing it when it is believed to have happened. It appears to us now as an inferred event.

One of *Hubble*'s photos of the Carina nebula appears with the article. It is a lovely swirling of red-browns, light blues, and violets, with a yellow whirl emanating yellow, green, and brown off to the left. Here and there are bright white sparkling dots. Some dark areas provide contrast. It is beautiful. I can see faces in it and a horse. Actually, on the yellow whirl there seems to be a broken down city wall, or oil rigs. Last night I dreamed a woman was taking me shopping for truly fine clothing, and I glimpsed a scarf or wall hanging of many beautiful colors floating into one another. Compared to the *Hubble* picture, the reds in my dream were brighter and less brown, though they took up little space; the blues were more royal or lapis lazuli, and they contrasted more sharply with the red. I generally do not like to go shopping, but in this dream I was having a good time.

*Nebula* is a Latin word meaning "mist, vapour, cloud." (Kidd 1961: 213) A nebula may be diffuse, as "a cloudlike, luminous or dark mass composed of gases and small amounts of dust," or it may be planetary, as "a central star surrounded by a gaseous envelope," or yet it may be extragalactic, as "an exterior galaxy." (Stein 1984: 955) Perhaps a scientist might object that I see faces, a horse, or a city wall in a *Hubble* photo of the Carina nebula, insisting that in science I must withdraw my subjective idiosyncrasies. Science, after all, is an endeavor to be objective, to observe what anyone else could also see and not just what is particular for me. But even the colors I saw were specific to me; blind or color-blind people would not see what I saw. In fact, my view of a color may be at least slightly different from anyone else's view. Moreover, I distinguished left from right in viewing the image, thus voiding any claim to be impersonal, inasmuch as left and right depend upon an individual viewer. And I was able to see a somewhat similar and dazzling spread of color in a dream, without the use of any telescopic data or even my eyes.

Some mode of consciousness, whether vague or clear, is correlated with the appearance of the *Hubble* picture of the Carina nebula. A telescope does not, strictly speaking, have an appearance or even an image, for it does not see or perceive. It reflects and relays light. Seeing and perceiving in general are spontaneous intentional acts that carry a weight of meaning. As temporal acts, seeing and perceiving involve memory, attention, and expectation. Telescopes do not appear to do these acts. But the act of perceiving a picture from such a telescope does require intentional activity, even if the act is experienced as vague.

While astronomers and physicists hold standards of objectivity in their work, they nevertheless have to admit that perception and thinking constitute an essential part of science, and that science is a co-operative intentional accomplishment of subjectivity. Objectivity is an ideal sought by scientists. Astronomy itself depends upon strongly felt interest in stars, planets, and the origin of the universe. As Michael Polanyi says in his Preface to *Personal Knowledge: Towards a Post-Critical Philosophy*: "I have shown that into every act of knowing there enters a passionate contribution of the person knowing what is being known, and that this coefficient is no mere imperfection but a vital component of his knowledge." (Polanyi 1962: viii)

Like astronomists passionately interested in learning about the formation of galaxies in outer space, archaeologists try to learn about events far back in time as they study discovered relics. Ancient, if not original, objects compel the attention of both. They spend years of their lives observing, ordering, and describing minutely detailed data about what is immensely far away from the immediately perceived. More commonly, we see things everyday that we never go into, walk around, or observe from another perspective. Yet each ordinary thing has a possibly infinite series of possible perspectives from which it may be beheld. A building across the street from the YMCA window, behind which I regularly exercise on an elliptical machine, has four stories and a door on the roof which I never noticed explicitly until I had a dream about a row of shops I had often passed but never entered. I then looked at the building with more focus and remembered going up to the roof in a similar building in San Francisco and seeing the city in quite a new way.

Each object has other sides not given directly but only summarily, vaguely, or imaginatively. In a corresponding way, intentional acts also have indirectly given aspects, which Husserl has referred to as "horizons" or "horizon," in the plural to mean the scope of intentional acts, and in the singular to mean a limit or boundary that continually opens up the more we approach it. From William James, Husserl also called the indirectly given aspects "fringes," as I mentioned earlier. Husserl described a "*co-present* margin" or "continuous ring around the actual field of perception," as "a *dimly apprehended depth or fringe of indeterminate reality*." (Husserl 1958: 102)

Freud and Jung also recognized and appreciated the scope, the opening-up, the fringes, and/or the depth accompanying any focus of intentional life; they saw it as "energy," and they spoke of it as "the unconscious." In developing his sense of psychic energy, Jung took up Arthur Schopenhauer's fundamental sense of awareness as *Wille* that manifests itself as cause, force, stimulus, motive, ground, or sufficient reason. (Schopenhauer 1974: 6, 41–2, 67–71, 207–15) With this fundamental sense of awareness in mind, Jung then expanded Freud's sense of *libido* beyond its exclusively sexual definition. Jung did not want to ignore the many modes of psychic life which he found described not only by Schopenhauer, but also by Cicero, Augustine, and other classical authors who understood *libido* in many ways, such as want, wish, willful desire unbridled by reason, delight, striving, will, taking pleasure, proper concern, urge, lust, and appetite. (Jung 1976a: 128–31)

Jung thus saw awareness as a desiring, an energetic interest, a tending that in great part coincides with Husserl's sense of intending as tending towards meaning. Appealing to the etymology of *libido* as longing, eagerness, and love, Jung writes:

> Having once made the bold conjecture that the libido which was originally employed in the production of ova and spermatozoa is now firmly organized in the function of nest-building, for instance, and can no longer be employed otherwise, we are compelled to regard every striving and every desire, including hunger and instinct however understood, as equally a phenomenon of energy.
>
> This view leads to a conception of libido which expands into a conception of *intentionality* in general.
>
> (Jung 1976a: 137)

Jung then refers to an earlier quotation of his from Freud and continues:

> As the above quotation from Freud shows, we know far too little about the nature of human instincts and their psychic dynamism to risk giving priority to any one instinct. We would be better advised, therefore, when speaking of libido, to understand it as an energy-value which is able to communicate itself to any field of activity whatsoever, be it power, hunger, hatred, sexuality, or religion, without ever being itself a specific instinct. As Schopenhauer says: "The Will as a thing-in-itself is quite different from its phenomenal manifestation, and entirely free from all forms of phenomenality, which it assumes only when it becomes manifest, and which therefore affect its objectivity only, and are foreign to the Will itself."
>
> (Jung 1976a: 137)

Schopenhauer had spoken of Will as not only apparent or phenomenal but also as not apparent or not phenomenal, as beyond the horizon of awareness and existing "in itself." Of course, to speak of Will as not phenomenal is nevertheless to have it as apparent in some way, as indirect, marginal, or imagined. The sense of things as existing in themselves as distinct from their appearance to us is an inseparable part of their appearance to us. Things are given that way, as existing beyond our limited experience of them. While our own awareness that we are living now is self-apparent, it too is nevertheless incompletely given at any moment and so is thought of as "existing beyond the given, as in itself."

On the way to affirming his agreement with Schopenhauer, Jung observed that libido or consciousness appears in many modes, even as it appears as existing beyond or transcending any one of them. Jung conceived of psychic energy as "*intentionality* in general," and the italics are his. In this conception, Jung was emphasizing that tending toward meaning is an "energy-value" that can be expressed in a wide variety of intentional acts, for example, as commanding (power), longing (hunger), feeling (hatred), desiring (sexuality), or yearning to transcend (religion). In explicitly agreeing with Schopenhauer, Jung was affirming not only that intending is self-apparent as lived, but also that it exceeds our grasp of ourselves as subjects of intending. For the flow of awareness as tending toward any meaning is indeed a Will of its own, not under the deliberate direction of me or of us. In recognizing Will, we thus come to notice the distinction between what we call "ego," what is "up to us," and Will itself. Hence intentionality as it appears to us is necessarily double: it is its own Will or source of energetic interest, on one hand, while, on the other hand, it relates to, or provides energy for, a particular "me" in a variety of modes.

Unseen stellar constellations, ancient remnants, views of things from new perspectives, and even the transfinite may thus be present in the margins of awareness, animating and compelling our attention, insofar as they belong to Will as source of intending. These objects continuously remain beyond what appears directly. Their intentional existence is nevertheless actual and affective.

In confirming the exactness of my long quotation of Jung's lines above from *Symbols of Transformation* on libido, Freud, intentionality, and Schopenhauer, which I had previously typewritten into my manuscript, I went to Jung's book and found several inserted pages that a friend had copied and sent to me years ago from *The Symbolic Quest: Basic Concepts of Analytical Psychology* by Edward C. Whitmont. In these pages, Whitmont tells of

> one of Jung's earliest cases in which he describes the hallucinatory fantasy of an uneducated schizophrenic who at that time was hospitalized in Zürich. The patient used to call the hospital physicians to the window and inform them that if they looked at the sun and moved their heads from side to side they could see a tail or penis coming down from the sun and moving to and fro. This, he said, was the source of the wind.
>
> (Whitmont 1979: 74)

I found these sentences striking because, a day or two before, I had heard someone say something strange to me about a penis being so large that "you could hear air move." The speaker had never read Jung or Whitmont, and had not seen their books or copies of their pages.

Whitmont then reports that, after Jung's patient died, Jung was studying

> a German philologist's translation of a Mithras liturgy, from the original Greek papyrus which was then accessible only to a few scholars. In this obscure work dealing with Mithraic initiation it was stated that the initiate saw a pendulous tube coming down from the sun, from which arose the wind. The initiate was then asked to move his head to see the tube moving, producing the east and west winds. Jung added that there were other details in the text, as well as in the schizophrenic fantasy, and that his study of the fantasy helped him to understand some difficult passages in the text.
>
> (Whitmont 1979: 74)

A year after Jung's death, an article on the front page of *The New York Times* for October 11, 1962, attracted Whitmont's attention. The headline was "Mariner 2 Data Disclose a Constant Solar Wind." The article began: "The Mariner 2 spacecraft bound for a December 2 rendezvous with Venus has discovered that there is a steady wind of charged particles blowing off the boiling surface of the sun into interplanetary space." (Whitmont 1979: 75)

A year and one month later in *The New York Times* for November 11, 1963, there was a report under the headline "Comet Wags Tail in 4 Day Rhythm":

> Regular Movement May Be Linked with Solar Wind, Astrophysicists Assert/ Cyclic Action Puzzles/ Nothing is Known About Sun that Would Account for it/ There is a comet which slowly wags its tail. The wags have a rhythm, each taking about 4 days and covering a 15 degree arc. Nobody knows why they occur …. By wagging its tail, the comet may be telling scientists something about the solar wind, a cloud of electrons and atomic fragments spewed out continuously in all directions by the sun. The solar wind causes the comet's tail to stream outward always away from the sun, regardless of which direction the comet is moving.
>
> (Whitmont 1979: 75)

I did not remember these pages from Whitmont, with his references to *The New York Times*, when I became interested in the *Hubble* space telescope and started writing about it, as a prelude to writing more about intentionality and Will in Jung and Schopenhauer. The specific content that Jung's patient, the Mithras liturgy, and the two newspaper articles mentioned, and that I had heard spoken about briefly but accurately, was not something that the patient, the liturgy, the newspaper, or the speaker had learned from any of the others. Yet they all showed an awareness of the same detailed phenomenon. A content presented itself as "whole and complete, without our being able to explain or discover how this content came into existence." (Jung 1976b: 453) The content had the distinctive characteristic belonging to what Jung calls "intuition."

Although I cannot know directly, it seems that there is a fundamental constitutive intending that is going on, both as a Will of its own and as source for the meaning–intending of one or more individuals, that includes not only a present moment, but also the old and the distant, the other sides of things, the beginnings and the aims. While the nebulae appear as we study data from a telescope, nebulous horizons of awareness appear too as we study our own experience and find much that is given inexplicably yet "intuitively" in Jung's sense of the word. The libido as intentionality or Will that I was once again trying to write about expressed itself in a strange way and made itself partially apparent in my experience.

# Chapter 17

# The Other in us

As Husserl repeatedly turned his attention to the phenomena of awareness, so Jung gave much attention to dreams and to what he called "fantasy-images from the unconscious." Jung advised anyone who wanted to know the complex nature of his own personality to do the same. A student or analysand would need to discover that the actors and the plot in his dream or chain of fantasy "have some purposeful relationship to his conscious situation, that he is being addressed by the unconscious, and that *it* causes these fantasy-images to appear before him." (Jung 1977: 496) The man would have to face the negations, contradictions, or disapprovals in what was appearing before him, and "really have it out with his alter ego," (Jung 1977: 496) inasmuch as his ego is not the whole of his personality.

> This process of coming to terms with the Other in us is well worth while, because in this way we get to know aspects of our nature which we would not allow anybody else to show us and which we ourselves would never have admitted.
>
> (Jung 1977: 496)

Jung saw purposeful intending in dreams and fantasies. He respected the unconscious as "the Other in us" deliberately addressing us and causing phenomena to appear before us. Psychic energy for Jung was powerfully intentional as *Wille*, as cause, force, and ground of appearances. He recognized that the "Other" causes dreams and fantasies on purpose to present to us how it sees us. For how other people see us and how we see ourselves are far from sufficient for genuine self-knowledge. There are things we do not allow other people to show us and things we do not even want to admit to ourselves. So the unconscious brings these unpleasant things up, as "shadow" and opposite to the ego, generating an interesting tension in the personality that is an increase of psychic energy.

The opposition is much more than a simple binary "X and not X," inasmuch as there is an ancient Square of Opposition which shows twelve logical relations of dependence among statements, as I have explained elsewhere. (Tougas 2009) Fitting nicely on this Square are twelve erotic relations among Adept, Soror, Anima, and Animus, as distinguished by Jung. (Tougas 2009) Taking the shadow seriously is a long, complex, and sobering task which involves not only thinking but also feeling. Moreover, paying attention to one's own shadow in self-reflection is not a popular activity. Jung laments that, in the West, we do not seem to have time for self-knowledge or even think it is useful. "We believe exclusively in doing and do not ask about the doer, who is judged only by achievements that have collective value." (Jung 1977: 498) Meeting the shadow involves a kind of dying. But the unconscious will not yield up its energy for the whole personality without a price, a sacrifice, a recognition of its authority.

When the ego dies in even small ways, one compensation is an increase of awareness that the personality is much more than the ego, inasmuch it is grows from the deeper self, the little-known ground. An ego that realizes its limits does not have to waste time trying to be more than it is. Then it is better able to help express the whole whose meaning lies in the dim margins of awareness, in the unconscious that asks the ego to take part in the creative unfolding of the personality.

A willing ego does what nobody else can do in its place. When such an ego responds attentively to the self as other, the individual person evolves more energetically towards his or her *telos*, the living out of the meaning of his or her life. This goal is the specific essence of the individual and it is known nebulously though often forcefully. As Aristotle wrote in *Physics* 198a25, "the 'what' and 'that for the sake of which' are one." (Aristotle, trans. 1941: 248) The why of a thing is what it is; it exists in order to be itself. The *telos* and the essence are the same cause insofar as a thing acts in order to become and be what it is. When the ego adds the energy that it has to the unconscious intending of the meaning of the whole personality, the *telos* is felt with added intensity, it is symbolized with greater force, and the person stretches more fully into what he or she is.

Self-knowledge that is both a recognizing and a willing used to be a chief aim of philosophy and psychology before these pursuits became overshadowed by the method of natural science. Today, there is much public interest in natural, social, and cultural phenomena, but comparatively little scholarly attention to subjectivity as lived individually. People seem to believe that subjective phenomena are merely private, particular, and insignificant, especially when compared with quantifiable masses of data. But great quantities of what is fundamentally insignificant do not make for significance. An individual subject has irreplaceable value. Groups and populations have worth on the basis of the individuals constituting them. Moreover, the world as a whole is a dependent whole: it is inseparable from subjective experience. It is an appearing world. It is nothing alone and cannot be left alone.

As I said in Chapter 10 above, our time-consciousness is neither arbitrary nor private, nor is it a socially constructed product of an historical period. Rather, it is presupposed in and for any historical period. The most powerful historical forces still need time during which to exist. They exist in inseparable relation to succession and duration, to some kind of immanent experiencing, to the fullness of expectation, attention, and memory. They are non-independent of subjectivity.

Individual subjectivity seemed to be a speck of sand in the Milky Way, according to a scientific view, but when we notice the phenomena of awareness that put the world before us in a variety of ways, and when we study the intentional activity that continually goes on temporally, we are given a fullness of being that leads us back to a center. Galaxies, nebulae, ancient times, and we ourselves are linked back to a core, to what we cannot exist without: the work of spirit that underlies each moment of awareness and intends the phenomena we live.

# Part IV

# Work in progress

Part IV

Work in progress

# Chapter 18

# Analytical psychology

In analytical psychology today, there exists a popular belief that psyche is fantasy and experience is imaginal. Jung contributed to this belief insofar as he often spoke of his experience in terms of the unconscious, its images, and its symbols. But, as I have shown in Chapter 3, what Jung means by "images" is fundamentally what Husserl means by "phenomena": appearances of various kinds as given in experience.

Jung would have appreciated clarification from Husserl. He refers to Plato and Kant as he bemoans the fact that English translators often use the word "image" as equivalent in meaning to "idea" to name anything whatsoever that is before awareness. Thus, they use the word "idea" without distinguishing whether the term refers to a sensation or to a Platonic Idea. For British empiricists, awareness was constituted primarily by sense data, and secondarily by "images" as copies or "ideas." But these "ideas" are quite distinct from the ideals that drew the attention of Plato. Jung affirmed the distinction, but the confusion still exists in English translations. But if we speak of the "being in the soul" as a flow of phenomena or appearances of various kinds, which may be sensed, imagined, felt, thought—beheld as present in a variety of ways—we avoid confusion and keep from reducing awareness to one of its modes. It is important for anyone interested in analytical psychology to recognize phenomena for what they are and so avoid the presumption that phenomena are images. Phenomenological distinctions are important for analytical psychologists.

In his book *Jung and Phenomenology*, Roger Brooke aims to link insights of phenomenology to analytical psychology. (Brooke 1991) Brooke's sense of intentionality, however, is not informed by observation of actions and passions that tend toward meaning, and are to some degree fulfilled in perception of some kind. Instead, Brooke speaks of intentionality as "the ontological 'there' of world-opening which makes it possible for a thing to 'be' and consciousness to be appropriated as 'someone's.'" (Brooke 1991: 42–3) Brooke leaves out subjective characteristics of intending, such as desire, attraction, and interest. His spatial description has no reference to ways in which a thing, consciousness, and the world are lived and felt in experience. He does not seem to notice that objects are present as meant and perceived in some way, and that meaning and perceiving involve subjects. Moreover, Brooke considers Jung's introverted attitude to be a disaster and calls any trace of it "Cartesianism" inasmuch as it is a directed interest in subjectivity.

Jung's approach to subjectivity in analysis is an involvement that intensifies the experience of a personal individual while different sides of the problem being suffered are discriminated and endured until something new and unexpected comes to be. Far from splitting a subject away from others, such personal involvement reveals that both the client and the analyst are closely related to the world at large, as parts of a whole to which they bear some equivalence. Jung knows that personal subjectivity is different from impersonal objectivity, but when Brooke finds Jung admitting this distinction, Brooke accuses Jung of unsound theory. (Brooke 1991: 168) He persists in his judgment of Jung to the end of his book. Thus Jung looks bad. But even worse is the attitude Brooke demonstrates towards analysis. He believes that his personal presence in an analytical situation is not his own, but is rather, as he admits, "the embodied amplification of an image." (Brooke 1991: 168)

Brooke affirms that images, not phenomena, are primary. For him, awareness is a flow of images, not of appearances of various kinds. He believes that intentionality is fantasy; he does not observe its tending toward meaning, its desire for presentation, its seeking for experience as fulfillment of meaning. He seems to limit subjectivity to impersonal forces and spatial situations. Accordingly, his view of analysis denies the importance of personal presence. Without appearing ashamed, Brooke turns to James Hillman for support in being an amplification of an image and says:

> Don't make too sharp a distinction between the relationship to the analyst and the relationship to the world of images. After all, the analyst – and the patient, too – are images in the world of images, are enacting fantasies. I just prefer to start with the fantasy rather than with the person, that's all.
>
> (Brooke 1991: 65)

Brooke and Hillman see phenomena as merely images. Thus they remain with representations without acknowledging the existence of presentations of reality in a wide variety of lived experiences. They fail to examine intentionality; they only imagine it. Their belief has consequences for their analytical practice: they give primary attention to images and downplay personal involvement through other intentional modes, such as empathy, memory, and expectation.

The most therapeutic element I experienced in my first analysis was the genuinely personal presence of the analyst herself, before whom I was myself and took responsibility for my life. My analyst liked images, but she was no mere image, any more than I was, and we both knew it. We suffered together as individuals. Her compassion and endurance were no fantasy.

Jung's attitude toward life and human affairs contrasts sharply with that of Hillman and his followers. Jung describes himself in relation to Nietzsche:

Nietzsche had lost the ground under his feet because he possessed nothing more than the inner world of his thoughts – which incidentally possessed him more than he it.... he succumbed to exaggeration and irreality. For me, such irreality was the quintessence of horror, for I aimed, after all, at *this* world and *this* life. No matter how deeply absorbed or how blown about I was, I always knew that everything I was experiencing was ultimately directed at this real life of mine. I meant to meet its obligations and fulfill its meanings.

(Jung 1961: 189)

We do not experience evidentially that imagining is the only intending there is. For to give evidence that imagining is the only intending would be to perform another kind of intentional act besides imagining and hence to show that imagining is not the only kind of intending there is. Indeed, imagining depends on direct experience of what is perceived as present in some way, and perception in turn depends upon a new now as continually arising, without which there is no temporal flux. Awareness depends upon a spontaneity that can hardly be named, that is other to us, even as it constitutes our experiences through which this moment, the world, and we ourselves are present now, and again now. There is a sustaining intent beyond our deliberate purposes. Any assumption that tries to explain it, be it an image-personification theory of imaginal psychology or a causal theory of science, is secondary, derivative, and indirect; the assumption depends for its existence on the very presence that it is trying to account for.

Moreover, after a painstaking summary and perceptive analysis of Hillman's basic "archetypal" viewpoint, W. A. Shelburne finds that Hillman appears not to be open to criticism outside the circle of his fundamental assumptions:

For in purporting to offer a depth psychological critique of all experience in terms of the theory of archetypes (cf. Hillman, *Re-Visioning Psychology*, pp. 132–3), Hillman is moving toward a theory that does not take seriously any criticism which does not accept the perspective of archetypes. For such criticism can be "psychologised" and reduced to its archetypal elements, and thus used as a supporting datum for that which it would criticize.

(Shelburne 1984: 36)

Shelburne notices that, while Hillman "sees-through" his own position as being just one more fantasy, "it appears that his views are really meant to be understood as definitive ones." (Shelburne 1984: 36) Reflecting critically on one's own position, however, calls for more than fantasizing. Other kinds of noticing are required.

Plato had a sign on the gate of his Academy that said in Greek: let no one enter here who does not know mathematics. Having a calculator on hand was not a guarantee of admission. Plato meant that a person must experience and distinguish sense data, images, perceptual data, logical evidence, and mathematical beholding, in order to begin to recognize the Just, the Good, and the Beautiful as ideals. Maybe one could get into the Academy with only part of the task accomplished. But Plato meant that it is important to proceed from images and sensations to argument and dialogue, in which one ironically comes to know one's ignorance. In such poverty and hunger, one begins to practice some mathematical beholding. Observing numbers and the Equal makes it evident that astounding aspects of reality do exist, no less than sensate things. And the soul is akin to them all.

Analytical psychologists do not necessarily have to read Plato, yet they stand to gain from a study of the concept of the least transfinite number which is indicated by the symbol $\aleph_0$. Imperfectly grasping this concept is a remarkable experience and provides a clearer sense of continuum and infinite series. Then the flow of phenomena in awareness can be noticed more evidently for what it is: a double continuity holding infinite series of infinite series in which we all are related. When an analyst understands and feels the significance of the flow of time, admiration and awe can then replace a tendency to make narrow assumptions that would deny the fundamental incomprehensibility of awareness. Attention can then be given to the remarkable presence of self and other in a continuum, in various intentional modes.

# Chapter 19

# Animus in a woman

One is not alone: there is another. Self and other are two. What is the cause of there being two? This is a philosophical question that Socrates raised in *Phaedo* 96e–97b. (Plato, trans. 1963: 78–9) He was puzzled as he realized that both adding and dividing are causes of two. One added to another surely make two. But one can be divided into two. Of course, one apple and one apple are two apples; one apple cut in half makes two half-apples. But two exists in both situations.

Analysis involves two: self and other, as client and analyst, are put together. But self and other also appear in each individual as a whole. A noticing of two in an individual may and should occur in analysis, for both partners. For a woman, the recognition of two inseparable aspects involves a discriminating power that Jung calls "animus," the masculine other as inseparable part of a feminine self. (Jung 1979: 14) The Latin noun *animus* is masculine and it means "mind, soul; consciousness; reason, thought, opinion, imagination; heart, feelings, disposition; courage, spirit, pride, passion; will, purpose; term of endearment." (Kidd 1961: 21) I often translate this Latin word as "spirit."

For a man, the two are noticed not so much by discrimination or division but rather by addition or reunion. The feminine other as inseparable part of a masculine self is called "anima," from Latin noun *anima* which is feminine and means "wind, air; breath; life; soul, mind; ghost, spirit." (Kidd 1961: 21) I often translate this Latin word as "soul."

The masculine other in a woman herself is not identical to the masculine as it appears in a man. For a woman, since her birth, has a likeness to her mother that a man does not have, and so she has both femininity and masculinity in ways that are different from the ways in which a man has them, as I say in an article published in *Harvest*. (Tougas 2000) While a woman may learn much about masculinity from men and the surrounding world, her masculine aspect is not simply added to her from family, culture, and society as she grows up. Animus cannot be completely accounted for as a social construction, made by others, insofar as "this spirit is itself a creative source and it helps bring the woman's own individuality into being." (Tougas 2000: 56)

Animus is a noticing directed at the woman's intentional life as arising spontaneously from an unknown yet deeply felt source. It is a focusing power that brings to her attention the otherness of awareness, as ground for her own purposive action and deliberate choices. Thus it enables her to distinguish that she is two. In becoming aware of this two-sided interdependency, she becomes aware of the distinguishing energy itself as a contrast from the reciprocity of the two. For the distinguishing energy is sharp, clear, determinate, and explicit, while her original relation with mother and the unknown source is fluid, ongoing, embracing, and implicit. The distinguishing is something different from the original feminine that appears in the self-reflection whereby she counts that she is two, and so then, in continuing to distinguish, she counts the something different as three.

If, however, a woman identifies with her animus, she loses her standpoint as one aspect of the triad. Or if she hears and uncritically believes the opinion of some psychologists that the self or intentional ground of a woman is masculine "insofar as her ego is feminine and she has to carry the opposite gender somehow 'in her unconscious,'" her failure to reflect makes her identify animus with ground and so forget the relation of the feminine two. (Tougas 2000: 61) Accordingly, a woman needs to respond actively and accept the tendency to focus, sort out, and distinguish—exercising this tendency even in "small" details. For this power to discriminate what is distinct yet inseparable is an aspect of spirit that helps create her.

Animus is thus not a distinct intentionality of its own kind, but is rather an intensification of perceiving, hoping, remembering, dreaming, feeling, and other kinds of intending. Its energy is focused, assertive, and reflective. It attracts the woman's attention and, like a partner, enables her to notice what she is doing, experiencing, and living. It gives her strength and flexibility of mind so that she is able not only to envision what at first seemed strange, but is also able to venture and carry out what she envisions.

A well-directed animus is like a father who not only teaches his daughter how to conduct her life in a man's world, but who also affirms her connection to mother. For a man, however, the anima is a force that captures his attention and turns him back towards the intentional source from which he distinguished himself at an early age, just as he was separating himself from his mother. In growing up, a man tends to differentiate himself from others, distance himself from his feelings, develop abstract systems, and calculate how to live by them. "When he says 'I' and lives out what he means, he manifests spirit as a heated intensity of focus, as an urgency to make distinctions and count parts in the continuum of life." (Tougas 2000: 64) He says "I do this," and he indeed does, but he is often unaware of the deeper intentionality that provides the meaning and the energy for his doing. Inasmuch as he forgets what he is non-independent of, he needs to be reminded of the necessary relation he has to what constitutes his awareness and his subjectivity. Hence, anima for him is not the differentiating power of animus, for he already has enough of that. Rather, anima is an attraction that draws him back into relation with what his sharp focus obscured: an implicit connection with what is other to ego, what is other to the "I" he lives and does. When he comes to feel his essential dependence on a deeper intentionality that he cannot control, he remembers that it exists after all, and so he comes to be freed from the loneliness that accompanies separation.

Husserl did not know of Jung's use of the terms "animus" and "anima." Yet he surely recognized the courageous and bright philosophical spirit of Edith Stein and her accurate perception of what another person was feeling, as quotations from Stein's autobiography have shown in Chapters 4 and 12 above. As also noted in Chapters 4 and 6, Stein had a spirit that helped her affirm a wide sense of existence—of not only the sensate, but also the logical, the felt, the remembered, the hoped for. A strong force impelled Stein—a desire for knowledge, an amazement at the power of thinking. For her, *logos,* the ability to express meaning in words, was bound up with strong passion, bodily energy, and compelling demand.

In the last events recounted in her memoirs, as I indicated Chapter 12, Stein's self was apparent, the self that was the turning-point of her whole personality. Through Husserl, Stein came to see the fundamental worth of the power constituting her, although she probably knew this power much more in January, 1939, while completing her recollection of events, than she had understood herself in 1916. Husserl was a likeness to her animus. Thus, she was not wholly dependent upon him for knowing herself, as her own spirit by its trials and challenges was awakening and enabling her to know herself and her life's direction—that long way upon which she had been tending since she had first gone to Göttingen, and by which she now had arrived at the convent in Echt, where she was completing her autobiography. Remembering in detail the main events of her life years afterwards, and feeling their significance in new ways, gave Stein access to a deeper level of her subjectivity through the intensifying focus of animus.

Had he heard specifically about "animus" or "anima," Husserl would have asked: "How is it given? In what experience is it present?" I can begin to address these questions by recalling and describing a dream experience I had of being shown an activity in myself. I briefly glimpsed a moment of my intentional life as a formative aiming that was working to put meaning before me in awareness, as noted earlier in Chapter 11 and as recorded right after the dream experience.

After much intense writing about time and subjectivity, I had gone to sleep. In my sleep, I was thinking about the Latin words *magister* and *magistrātus*: they were coming up before me, both in meaning and in print. Something in me was wanting to have the right meaning before me, as both correct and elegant, with beauty and simplicity. In the dream, something in me was seeking to produce a correct meaning, to put it before me in perception and in print, as though on a stage, with frugality. There is an intending toward meaning going on in me, and very early that morning I caught a glimpse of its effort, of its going towards something before me, as if putting it together and going through possibilities to get the right one there. I briefly saw and remember an active intending going on of itself, as part of a dream in my sleep, as seeking and looking for just the right thing to aim attention at, arranging and pulling out what is to be there. I awoke slowly with an urgent sense to remember this intending and to try to describe it in words.

In recording the dream, I thought about the word *magister, -tri*, m., male teacher. I had not been dreaming of the word *magistra, -ae*, f., female teacher, referring to myself as a teacher or to another female Latin teacher I know. Rather, the word had meant "male teacher," which still recalls to me the inner teacher Augustine spoke of, the recollection that Plato saw as the core of learning, and the animus or spirit in woman that Jung observed in women around him. In this dream, animus or spirit as male teacher enabled me to notice intending as it was happening.

As I said earlier in Chapter 11, this teacher is not a city official, *magistrātus*. What teaches me in this way is not a public power. Through its presence in a dream, I have evidence of spirit at work as other in the arising of the now moment of awareness as a putting of phenomena before me.

In German "to put before" is *vorstellen*; in Kant's philosophy, *Vorstellung* means what is put before consciousness, a presentation of something to awareness as well as a representation akin to presentations on a stage. I explained Kant's use of this word in Chapter 3 while comparing Husserl and Jung with respect to their terms for the being in the soul; at that time I noted that Kant used the term *Vorstellung* as a heading for various kinds of "appearance," including *Idee*. In Chapter 9, I said that in 1871 Cantor had already had what he called a *Vorstellung* or presentation of a transfinite ordinal number, as a definitely infinite order. Yet he did not refer to it even in 1880, nine years after the first glimpse; at last, in articles published in 1887 and 1888, and in a little book in 1890, Cantor had enough confidence and insight to express what had appeared to him mathematically. In Chapter 14 on dreaming, I described dreaming as *Vorstellung* in two senses of the term, as both presentation and representation. Phenomena or appearances come before us in a variety of ways, as Kant, Husserl, Jung, Cantor, and a dream have shown me with the help of animus as focusing and intensifying power.

Another example of the experience of what can be called "animus" is given in Chapter 13 when, in relation to a Chinese fairy tale, a student's drawing of a mirror shows not only a woman, but also a man. In the reflection are the woman and her masculine strength as he is coming to her attention, just before his animating energy brings her to her senses, affirms the importance of her baby, and saves their lives. His persistent affirming and intelligent valuing of her "only one life" are just what she needs and just what he provides. He is in her own reflection just as she is in it, for he is enabling her to see herself as a whole. When she too affirms herself through the vigor of his intent, she begins to hope and her life can continue. In paying attention to the wider view of self he makes possible, the young woman comes to see and trust what might be, or could be, or ought to be.

I have been pointing out examples of the presence of animus in parts of this writing. I now want to add a description of two instances of the experiencing of what can be called "anima" in a man.

One summer, many years ago, an eminent male colleague at the Husserl Circle listened to my paper on subjectivity and internal time-consciousness. He affirmed that my understanding of Husserl was correct, but asked why the now moment as original and constitutive was subjective; could it not simply be an automatic process? I was aghast, but did not say much because I was nearly the only woman in the room. I think I said something like, "The now that bears meaning is felt, suffered, lived," but I did not convince him. A distinguished Husserlian scholar, he nevertheless implied that awareness was just like everything else; it was not life, spirit, or soul, for theoretically these were outdated notions. He spoke to other men about what ought to be most important as though he were talking about car mechanics or computer operations. He did not glimpse the infinite or the eternal in the new now, the origin "point" of awareness. He did not find it remarkable that our whole study, not to mention our existence, depends upon the presence of continuity as actually existing. Highly ranked as he was, he did not believe that he had a soul or that fundamentally he was soul and spirit. At least I knew that something was missing in his stance because my father and grandfathers had faith in the soul and showed great respect for the soul's commands. In this instance of my colleague's experience, anima was what he was overlooking and denying in refusing to acknowledge what he was depending on.

In contrast, Husserl recognized an animating energy that was powerful enough to enable him to live in the world, as I said at the beginning of Chapter 8. Moreover, Husserl wrote: "I have chosen my problems myself and have gone my own ways ... I have acted this way not in order to be virtuous, but from a compelling necessity." (Spiegelberg 1965: 89–90) He experienced an authority that gave him life and that also gave him a mission, as he said in German at his seventieth birthday celebration. (Husserl 1968: 161) At that celebration, he also said: "*Ich habe gar kein Verdienst.*" I have hardly merited anything. (Husserl 1968: 161) He was not trying to be virtuous or meritorious; rather, he was grabbed by the infinite and did not refuse to acknowledge it. Like the members of the Cultural Society in Vienna on May 7, 1935, Husserl struggled not to be suffocated but rather to find spirit as living breath and air, as I mentioned in Chapter 15. The Latin noun *anima* is feminine and means "wind, air; breath; life; soul, mind; ghost, spirit." (Kidd 1961: 21) What Husserl could not live without was the personal anima that made soul present to him through his heartfelt response in a lifetime of daily effort.

I have read Edith Stein's autobiography and so have grounds to affirm that Husserl was a likeness to her animus. Although Husserl did not write an autobiography, I nevertheless make bold now to affirm that Stein was a likeness to his anima. As evidence for this affirmation, I bring back a scene as given in Chapter 12:

> At that point we were just crossing over the Dreisam. The Master stood stock still in the middle of the *Friedrichsbrücke* and exclaimed in delighted surprise: "You want to help me? Yes! With you, I would enjoy working!"
>
> I do not know which one of us was more elated. We were like a young couple at the moment of their betrothal. In the Lorettostrasse, Frau Husserl and Erika stood watching us.

Husserl said to his wife: "Think of it! Fräulein Stein wants to come to be my assistant."

Erika looked at me. We needed no exchange of words to reach an understanding. Her deep-set, dark eyes were alight with intense joy. That night when we went to bed she said, "Good night, Lady Assistant!"

(Stein 1986: 411)

The elation of Husserl and Stein was like that of a young couple at the moment of their engagement. His wife and Stein's good friend were watching, but no one is described as being embarrassed or shocked. The joy was erotic, but was not expressed physically. The mutual promise was to collaborate in philosophical work.

Yet, as I noted subsequently in Chapter 12, the two did not collaborate. While Husserl responded in an original, personal way to the call of anima, it was more difficult for him to respond to an actual young woman and to develop an original way to work with her, given the social strictures of the times and the intense intimacy involved in conversing honestly about another's feeling as well as one's own. Nevertheless, it is evident that Husserl had great feeling for Stein and recognized that he had much to learn from her. To affect him so deeply, Stein must have been a likeness to his anima.

# Chapter 20

# Child analysis and the dark mother

In the first chapter of this book, I speak of a time in my life when soul and spirit were present to me "mostly in dreams. For many years after his death, the children's father appeared in my dreams, and we both changed over the years. I recorded my dreams whether big or small, and I participated in Jungian analysis."

I entered analysis the first time with a woman because I needed help in divorcing, raising small children, and finding work. I had to mature and form new attitudes. I was attracted to Jungian analysis because I had many dreams. I entered analysis the second time with a man because I needed help in surviving as a woman in academia and in continuing my own philosophical study.

When I first met the woman in a free initial session, I felt right away that she would be a person with whom I could work and be myself. Later, I learned that she originated and organized child studies programs at the C. G. Jung Institute, Boston and attended conferences in Europe. She invited child analysts from England, France, Switzerland, Italy, and western parts of the USA to give workshops for analysts, teachers, and anyone interested in adolescents and children. I attended some of them and was especially moved by Kaspar Kiepenheuer and Edith Sullwold. Around that time I read Irene Claremont de Castillejo, Sylvia Brinton Perera, M. Esther Harding, Dora M. Kalff, Marie-Louise von Franz, and C. G. Jung. I liked these studies and even thought of becoming an analyst.

My analyst saw adults in her home and children in a small office called "The Child's i." Near the end of that analysis, I went there and made a sand tray. I was afraid because I did not know how to do it or what to expect. "Good," she said. Afterwards she took pictures of my work and gave me a few. The prominent toy in the sand tray was a duck standing upright with wings like arms and a red-orange gash down the chest. The duck was facing a small white bird cage on whose top I had placed a typing keyboard which I had made with blue clay. The bird was about to write on the keyboard through which the caged bird was singing. I went out and bought Maya Angelou's book, *I Know Why the Caged Bird Sings*, and a word processor, my first computer. Our analytical meetings ceased and I later started meeting with my second analyst. I applied for and won a small grant which allowed me to have sabbatical leave. I gave my working hours each day to writing.

In making a sand tray there is little talk. Attention is involved in what figures, toys, or objects are being chosen and what is being made or destroyed in the sand. Sense perception, feeling, and guessing were going on, to be sure. Although I knew that my analyst studied Jung, attended classes, met with colleagues, wrote papers, and received supervision, and although I was attending workshops and reading Jung, I did not feel that she was understanding me through a system of concepts that took priority over her actual experience of observing me. Concepts strengthened her understanding and helped her knit together what she noticed and felt, but I rarely knew about them explicitly. She accepted what was given in a variety of modes of being given, aware that there are limits in each mode. Her alert and inquiring manner reminded me of Husserl's basic principle, which I quoted in Chapter 3: "*whatever presents itself in 'intuition' in primordial form* (as it were in its bodily reality), *is simply to be accepted as it gives itself out to be,* though *only within the limits in which it then presents itself.*" (Husserl 1958: 92, emphasis in original)

Jackie Schectman was my first analyst. To me, her greatest help was her wanting me to grow, mature, and become myself, a wanting which was inter-locked with a tending or striving that I was becoming aware of as part of myself. Through her, I experienced both the good mother and the bad mother, not only in her, but also in me. I could no longer be naïve and pretend I was responsible for only good things.

Early in the analysis, I told of a dream about my friend Elissa, who had died. I had met Elissa when we both were singing in a choir. She loved music and had recently been divorced from a cellist. She told me about living one day at a time, asking for help, and looking to a power greater than herself. She had lived in big cities and loved Paris. She died from a stroke at the age of forty-nine. I had the dream of Elissa a while after her death. After telling it to my analyst, I said (for I had read some psychology) that Elissa was a symbol that represented an aspect of self. At that point my analyst frowned, shook her head, and vehemently said, "No, no. Elissa is there. She is present. Why is she there? What does she want to say to you?" My flimsy explanation dissolved and I started to cry. I was moved that Elissa had taken the trouble to be present to me in a time of trouble; she was there to help me. She did give me strength and insight. From then on, I did not pretend that I knew what a dream experience was. I accepted it as it was given, though when I woke up, I did also accept the fact that I had been dreaming. I did not deny Elissa's presence, nor did I reduce it to the presence of the analyst. I was able to understand that there are different kinds of existence and there are limits to the ways in which each kind is given. Jackie and I did not expect to see Elissa on the street or in a choir. Elissa was indeed dead, and it was incomprehensible how she could come to me. But we accepted that we were living with the incomprehensible.

If I had not been in analysis with Jackie and had not let my presuppositions about dreaming as merely symbolic and representational be destroyed, I probably would have died. For I would have lost the source that was sustaining me day by day. I would have despaired more than I ever did as a teenager. I would not have ventured to write a book about phenomena.

Besides enabling me to accept more freely the reality given in dreaming, analysis with Jackie also enabled me to recognize and accept the dark, bad, or bereaved mother as a state of mind, not only in myself and in her, but also in our mothers and other women. Jackie wrote a book called *The Stepmother in Fairy Tales: Bereavement and the Feminine Shadow* which includes a chapter on the fairy tale "Hansel and Gretel." (Schectman 1993: 51–78) In that tale, there are two wicked stepmothers: one repeatedly abandons her children in the woods, and the other draws children into her overly sweet gingerbread house in order to fatten them up and then eat them.

An angry woman is probably the thing that men fear most. Society and psychology put the blame for many evils on the bad mother. Yet, as Jackie's observations show, such women are grieving, overlooked, impoverished, abused, unsupported. The stepmother who abandoned her children in the forest was honest about the situation of poverty and did not deceive her children about the dire necessity they faced. In throwing them out of the house and into the world, she was forcing them to turn to their own inner resources, as children who are "close to nature, close to the unconscious." (Schectman 1993: 52)

The stepmother in the gingerbread house with the oven ready to cook the children affected me most. I came to see that the woman who is overly nice soon will be among the depleted women, as she cannot please everyone. She can continue to keep up the sugary façade only by replenishing her energies with a meal of cooked children. She feeds off the younger ones she should be letting go. At an early age, Hansel and Gretel learn to see through her falsity. Captured in her house, they form an ingenious plan to go along with her until the time when, as the witch is putting Hansel into the oven, Gretel pushes the witch in instead.

What a relief not to have to pretend I was all nice! I was able to let my children go because I feared eating them. Failing in marriage forced me to turn to the resources of dreaming, analysis, and study. Because I was poor, I had to work hard and so found increasingly better jobs over the years. I would never have done these things out of a desire to be purely good or to earn merit. I *had to*. Necessity is a mother. I answered yes.

I also asked about Mother Nature as a philosophical problem: is Mother Nature a bad mother—is the source of life essentially evil? Jackie's work with me helped form the answer I felt in my heart. Moreover, in her book she specifically addresses the view of Melanie Klein, who sees the child as inherently sadistic. (Klein 1960: 185) For Klein, the child wishes to be a cannibal in relation to the mother; when her resources are depleted, the child senses the deprivation and demands even more. "These are times of great inner need, the moments when Dark Mother and Devouring Child meet face to face," Jackie acknowledges (Schectman 1993: 54), considering such moments of response to real devastation in life. And D. W. Winnicott (1965), also demurring from Klein, nonetheless affirms that in the mother–infant relationship, one can now and then discern a robust though usually implicit component of aggression, which may even seem to intend total destruction. When I imagine either a mother or a child killing the other, I experience a horrible feeling of total destruction and complete loss of trust; I tremble in fear, dizzy on the edge of an infinite abyss. Yet my very agitation attests to my having already known this abyss in some form. Winnicott sees a benign necessity in the mother's and infant's imagining that they have survived such destruction. He does so because this repeated moment furthers the infant's development of concern, which must reach beyond primitive inner impulsion toward more advanced forms of mutuality.

Accordingly, Jackie describes a sand tray of a seven-year-old boy who placed a big-breasted Buddha in the middle. After adding other objects, he destroyed them all with a small army tank. Then he locked away the tank and put the objects back upright.

> He removed the adult figures, and placed a white, Wise-Old-Man figure next to the motherly looking Buddha. He'd judged his personal parents, and disposed of them; the Great Parents at the center would provide whatever warmth and wisdom he would find.
>
> (Schectman 1993: 57)

I remember that at the age of seventeen I was sad and depressed. I did not know that such feelings could be talked about. I came across writings of Søren Kierkegaard, a Danish philosopher who lived from 1813 to 1855. In particular his book, *The Sickness unto Death*, grabbed me. For there he distinguished several kinds of despair in relation to one another. The first kind was unconsciousness of being a self. But consciousness of being a self involved other kinds of despair. I spent hours and days reading Kierkegaard. I did not understand most of what I had read, but I knew it was about something crucially important. While I continued to feel sad, I nevertheless felt somewhat heartened because I saw the sadness was about something real. If I had only made it all up, then I was really crazy. As it was, I could bear with it for a while until I knew more. Similarly, the children and young people in analysis with Jackie must have felt hope and encouragement when working with her, even though there was a lot that they did not understand about life and their problems, because she understood that what they were struggling through was tremendously important, and she too was struggling with them.

Nevertheless, working with Jackie did not involve even a temporary acceptance of illusion. At the beginning of our work, I assumed she would be a confidante, like some of my women friends. No, we aren't friends, she said firmly and angrily; the relationship in analysis is peculiar. I felt disappointed and wronged. Yet I later understood she was right. There were times when I "went over a boundary" that exists in analysis. For example, early one morning when no one was around, just before one of my early morning sessions, I planted some of my extra tomato plants in the yard in front of her apartment, as a surprise "gift" for her in the city.

No, that was intrusive; who was I to cross the fence and do the work of gardeners who cared for the place? I had not asked her beforehand. Moreover, as she made me realize, I had recently been intrusive and had crossed a boundary in gardening for a neighbor of mine. I was tremendously embarrassed. But Jackie was right. So I was amazed at what happened the last time I saw her.

Jackie stopped breathing on September 15, 2005. The last time I visited her was two months before, at the Jewish Home for the Aged in Dorchester. After the analysis had ended, I would visit her from time to time. When I came into her room, she was listening to a book on tape. She could no longer see with her outer eyes. She spoke animatedly about the things we usually spoke about, though she did not say much about her illness. When it was time for me to go, I gave her a hug and a kiss on the cheek; after the analysis was over, we had usually only hugged in a friendly way at the end of a visit. This time, I didn't know why but I kissed her cheek. Yet after I heard she had died, I was glad I had followed instinct. In the face of death we were reduced, or raised, to a different level: we were two human beings. And I was grateful to her for her toughness.

I had not dreamed of Jackie for a long time, but after recalling our analysis, rereading parts of her book, and now writing about her work, I dreamed of her last night. I had come down to Boston again to see her and she was living in a much classier place, more in town, in a place like a hotel. I go in and there is an area of darkness to the right. But there she is, the way she used to look before she got sick with diabetes—bouncy, smiling, and glowing; she is glad to see me and welcomes me. I look to the darkness and don't see her for a moment. Then I look back and see she is still smiling. She motions with her hand for me to come in farther and we go towards her place. I look at her and can't take my eyes off her eyes—they are bright blue, glowing, lapis lazuli eyes—and I am awed. She smiles and they glow. I am very glad to see her, even so briefly. I would not have seen her in this dream if I had despaired of the reality of dreaming long ago.

Seeing the mother in the light and the dark involves a rock bottom, ground level awareness that reminds me of Husserl's fundamental noticing that continually new appearances have an origin, "a point of actuality, primal source point, that from which springs the 'now,' and so on.... For all this, names are lacking." (Husserl 1964: 100) A seven-year-old boy making a sand tray with Jackie Schectman wordlessly put the Great Parent figures at the center. In this book, I have often noted with words that the phenomena of awareness originate in an incomprehensible source from which they are given, not made by us. We are its children, and in the time given to us we are asked to grow up.

I could not have written this book without a second analysis, in part because it too supported my awareness of dreams. During many years of analysis with a man, I regularly dreamed of my children's father whom I had met while we were philosophy students at Duquesne University. When we became engaged, he said that we would marry, have children, teach, and write, and later in life we would move to a house far away in the country "and do real, contemplative philosophy." But, like Husserl and Stein, we failed to collaborate. Much worse than they, we separated in an unfortunately difficult divorce. And yet, during the first decade after his death, I noticed in dreams that the children's father was changing. He was becoming kinder. In nearly every dream, he was taking care of our children, who were still growing up. We were still following the visitation arrangements whereby they would go from one home to the other at different times. In the dreams, he seemed to have them a lot of the time. Moreover, he was still a philosopher; our friends in graduate school had called him "Harry the Transcendental." He seemed to remain in the background of my writing. A few months ago, just before the proposal for this book was accepted, I dreamed that the things in his house were packed up, and I was there briefly and spoke to him warmly. In another dream around this time, maybe even before, I dreamed that he died. For a long time afterwards I did not dream of him.

Moreover, in the analysis with a man, I have not only been listened to and thought about, but have also heard bits about history, and current scholarly and cultural matters seemingly extraneous to my immersion in high school teaching. My analyst surely has wanted to remind me that there is a larger life than the one I for a time felt was constraining me. And, in expressing his thoughts as they come to mind, he has also surely meant to enhance our sense that our interaction is open to the new and unexpected, a state which may serve analysis in a very positive way. Indeed, a life-transforming experience of openness was the theme of a story he told me about Charlie Parker in around his eighteenth year. In Parker's words:

> I remember one night before [going to] Monroe's I was jamming in a chili house on Seventh Avenue between 139th and 140th. It was December, 1939. Now I'd been getting bored with the stereotyped changes that were being used all the time at the time, and I kept thinking there's bound to be something else. I could hear it sometimes but I couldn't play it.
>
> Well, that night, I was working over *Cherokee,* and, as I did, I found that by using the higher intervals of a chord as a melody line and backing them with appropriately related changes, I could play the thing I'd been hearing. I came alive.

(Shapiro and Hentoff 1966: 354)

"Bird", "Yardbird", Charlie Parker was technically very skilled and knew Ray Noble's *Cherokee* inside out. That night he played it at a breakneck tempo to heighten the challenge to himself. "What he was playing for the first time was CHARLIE PARKER—this was a breakthrough to the musical form of his true self," my analyst told me. The way had been thoroughly prepared.

I had never heard *Cherokee* before, but the day after hearing my analyst speak of it, I happened to pick up a piece of paper on the floor. It was an album cover and listed on the notes was *Cherokee.* I found the compact disc, which did not belong to me, and listened to the tune for the first time, as played on guitar. I cannot explain how that paper got to be on the floor just at that time, nor why I picked it up. But the event happened after two years of my not being able to write, and three years besides of my not writing well enough, at a turning point when I suddenly saw and spoke for the first time about the meaning of this book as a whole. This was a breakthrough to the philosophical form of my true self. I understood myself as connected to the larger life, as a speaker in the public world of men. Had I not been taught week by week, had I not been fathered from a distance, even if imperfectly, to keep high standards of scholarship and culture, I would never have completed this book. I came alive.

# Bibliography

Angelou, M. (1969) *I Know Why the Caged Bird Sings*, New York: Bantam Books.

Aristotle (1941) *Metaphysics* and *Physics* in R. McKeon (ed.) *The Basic Works of Aristotle*, New York: Random House.

Atwood, G. E. and Stolorow, R. D. (1979) *Faces in a Cloud: Intersubjectivity in Personality Theory,* Lanham, Maryland: Jason Aronson Inc.

Augustine (1961) *Confessions,* trans. R. S. Pine-Coffin, Baltimore: Penguin Books.

Benjamin, J. (1988) *The Bonds of Love: Psychoanalysis, Feminism, and the Problem of Domination,* New York: Pantheon Books.

—(1998) *Shadow of the Other: Intersubjectivity and Gender in Psychoanalysis,* New York and London: Routledge.

Betteridge, H. T. (ed.) (1958) *The New Cassell's German Dictionary*, New York: Funk and Wagnalls Company.

Brooke, R. (1991) *Jung and Phenomenology,* London: Routledge.

Camus, A. (1995) *The First Man,* trans. D. Hapgood, New York: Alfred A. Knopf.

Cantor, G. (1955) *Contributions to the Founding of the Theory of Transfinite Numbers,* trans. P. E. B. Jourdain, New York: Dover Publications Inc.

Dauben, J. W. (1979) *Georg Cantor: His Mathematics and Philosophy of the Infinite*, Princeton: Princeton University Press.

De Castillejo, I. C. (1973) *Knowing Woman: A Feminine Psychology,* New York: Harper Colophon Books.

*The Economist* (2009) "Peek-a-boo," May 16, 2009.

Ellenberger, H. F. (1970) *The Discovery of the Unconscious: The History and Evolution of Dynamic Psychiatry,* New York: Basic Books, Inc., Publishers.

Giorgi, A. (2009) *The Descriptive Phenomenological Method in Psychology: A Modified Husserlian Approach,* Pittsburgh: Duquesne University Press.

Halling, S. (2008) *Intimacy, Transcendence, and Psychology: Closeness and Openness in Everyday Life,* New York: Palgrave Macmillan.

Harding, M. E. (1970) *The Way of All Women: A Psychological Interpretation,* New York: Harper and Row Publishers.

Hoffman, I. Z. (1998) *Ritual and Spontaneity in the Psychoanalytic Process: A Dialectical-Constructivist View,* Hillsdale, N. J.: Routledge and The Analytic Press, Inc.

Hugo, V. (1995) *Les Misérables,* Paris: Éditions Gallimard.

Husserl, E. (1958) *Ideas: General Introduction to Pure Phenomenology,* trans. W. R. B. Gibson, New York: The MacMillan Company.

—(1960) *Cartesian Meditations: An Introduction to Phenomenology*, trans. D. Cairns, The Hague: Martinus Nijhoff.

—(1964) *The Phenomenology of Internal Time-Consciousness*, trans. J. S. Churchill, Bloomington: Indiana University Press.

—(1966) *Husserliana X: Zur Phänomenologie des inneren Zeitbewusstseins (1893–1917)*, ed. R. Boehm, The Hague, Netherlands: Martinus Nijhoff.

—(1968) *Briefe an Roman Ingarden, Mit Erläuterungen und Erinnerungen an Husserl*, ed. U. Melle, The Hague, Netherlands: Martinus Nijhoff.

—(1970a) *The Crisis of European Sciences and Transcendental Phenomenology: An Introduction to Phenomenological Philosophy*, trans. D. Carr, Evanston: Northwestern University Press.

—(1970b) *Husserliana XII: Philosophie der Arithmetik, Mit ergänzenden Texten (1890–1901)*, ed. L. Eley, The Hague, Netherlands: Martinus Nijhoff.

—(1970c) *Logical Investigations, 2 vols*, trans. J. N. Findlay, New York: Humanities Press.

—(1977a) *La Crise de l'humanité Européenne et la philosophie: Die Krisis des Europäischen Menschentums und die Philosophie*, trans. P. Ricœur, Paris: Aubier Montaigne.

—(1977b) *Phenomenological Psychology: Lectures, Summer Semester, 1925*, trans. J. Scanlon, The Hague: Martinus Nijhoff.

Jung, C. G. (n.d.) *C. G. Jung: Letters, Vol. 2*, Princeton: Princeton University Press.

—(1961) *Memories, Dreams, Reflections*, trans. R. and C. Winston, New York: Pantheon Books.

—(1966–1992) *The Collected Works of C. G. Jung, 20 vols*, trans. R. F. C. Hull, ed. H. Read, M. Fordham, G. Adler, Princeton: Princeton University Press.

—(1966) *C. W. 7: Two Essays on Analytical Psychology.*

—(1969) *C. W. 8: The Structure and Dynamics of the Psyche.*

—(1976a) *C. W. 5: Symbols of Transformation.*

—(1976b) *C. W. 6: Psychological Types*, trans. H. G. Baynes, rev. R. F. C. Hull.

—(1977) *C. W. 14: Mysterium Coniunctionis.*

—(1979) *C. W. 9ii: Aion: Researches into the Phenomenology of the Self.*

—(1980) *C. W. 12: Psychology and Alchemy.*

Kalff, D. M. (1980) *Sandplay: A Psychotherapeutic Approach to the Psyche*, Boston: Sigo Press.

Kant, I. (1963) *Immanuel Kant's Critique of Pure Reason*, trans. N. K. Smith, London: Macmillan and Company Ltd.

Katz, R. (1964) *Axiomatic Analysis: An Introduction to Logic and the Real Number System*, Boston: D. C. Heath and Company.

Kidd, D. A. (ed.) (1961) *Collins Latin Gem Dictionary*, London: Collins.

Kiepenheuer, K. (1990) *Crossing the Bridge: A Jungian Approach to Adolescence*, trans. K. R. Schneider, La Salle, Illinois: Open Court Publishing Company.

Kierkegaard, S. (1941a) *Concluding Unscientific Postscript*, trans. D. F. Swenson and W. Lowrie, Princeton: Princeton University Press.

—(1941b) *Repetition: An Essay in Experimental Psychology*, trans. W. Lowrie, Princeton: Princeton University Press.

—(1954) *Fear and Trembling* and *The Sickness unto Death*, trans. W. Lowrie, Princeton: Princeton University Press.

Klein, M. (1960) *The Psychoanalysis of Children*, New York: Grove Press.

Landgrebe, L. M. (1980) "Husserl, Edmund," in *The New Encyclopaedia Britannica: Macropaedia, Volume 9*, Chicago: Encyclopaedia Britannica, Inc.

Leibniz, G. W. v. (1962) *Basic Writings: Discourse on Metaphysics, Correspondence with Arnauld, and Monadology,* trans. G. R. Montgomery, La Salle, Illinois: Open Court Publishing Company.

Nagel, E. and Newman, J. R. (1958) *Gödel's Proof,* New York: New York University Press.

Perera, S. B. (1981) *Descent to the Goddess: A Way of Initiation for Women,* Toronto, Canada: Inner City Books.

Plato (1963) *Phaedo* and *Timaeus* in E. Hamilton and H. Cairns (eds) *The Collected Dialogues including the Letters,* New York: Random House, Inc.

Polanyi, M. (1962) *Personal Knowledge: Towards a Post-Critical Philosophy,* Chicago: The University of Chicago Press.

Radhakrishnan, S. and Moore, C. A. (eds) (1957) *A Sourcebook in Indian Philosophy,* Princeton: Princeton University Press.

Russell, B. (1961) *The Basic Writings of Bertrand Russell,* New York: Simon and Schuster.

Saint John of the Cross (1959) *Dark Night of the Soul*, trans. E.A. Peers, Garden City, New York: Doubleday and Company, Inc.

Saint Teresa of Avila (1961) *Interior Castle,* trans. E. A. Peers, Garden City, New York: Doubleday and Company, Inc.

Schectman, J. M. (1993) *The Stepmother in Fairy Tales: Bereavement and the Feminine Shadow,* Boston: Sigo Press.

Schopenhauer, A. (1958) *The World as Will and Representation, 2 vols,* trans. E. F. J. Payne, New York: Dover Publications, Inc.

—(1974) *On the Fourfold Root of the Principle of Sufficient Reason,* trans. E. F. J. Payne, La Salle, Illinois: Open Court Publishing Company.

Seebohm, T. M. (1973) "Reflexion and Totality in the Philosophy of E. Husserl," *Journal of the British Society for Phenomenology,* 4 (1), 20–30.

Shapiro, N. and Hentoff, N. (eds) (1966) *Hear Me Talkin' to Ya: The Story of Jazz as Told by the Men Who Made It,* New York: Dover Publications, Inc.

Shelburne, W. A. (1984) "A Critique of James Hillman's Approach to the Dream," *Journal of Analytical Psychology,* 29, 35–56.

Spiegelberg, H. (1965; 2nd edn) *The Phenomenological Movement: A Historical Introduction,* The Hague: Martinus Nijhoff.

Stein, E. (1986) *Life in a Jewish Family, 1891–1916: An Autobiography,* trans. J. Koeppel, Washington, D.C.: ICS Publications.

—(1989; 3rd revised edn) *On the Problem of Empathy,* trans. W. Stein, Washington D.C.: ICS Publications.

—(1993) *Self-Portrait in Letters, 1916–1942,* trans. J. Koeppel, Washington, D. C.: ICS Publications.

Stein, J. (ed.) (1984) *The Random House College Dictionary,* revised ed., New York: Random House, Inc.

Stolorow, R. D., Atwood, G. E., and Brandchaft, B., (eds) (1994) *The Intersubjective Perspective,* Northvale, New Jersey: Jason Aronson Inc.

Stolorow, R. D., Brandchaft, B. and Atwood, G. E. (1995) *Psychoanalytic Treatment: An Intersubjective Approach,* London: Routledge.

Tougas, C. (2000) "What is the Difference between Spirit and Soul? Jungian Reflections," *Harvest: Journal for Jungian Studies,* 46 (1), 52–66.

—(2009) "Opposition and Postmodernism," *Jung Journal,* 3 (1), 68–77.

Tougas, C. T. and Ebenreck, S. (eds) (2000) *Presenting Women Philosophers,* Philadelphia: Temple University Press.

Von Franz, M.-L. (1972) *Patterns of Creativity Mirrored in Creation Myths,* Dallas, Texas: Spring Publications, Inc.

—(1983) *Shadow and Evil in Fairy Tales*, Dallas, Texas: Spring Publications, Inc.

Whitmont, E. C. (1979) *The Symbolic Quest: Basic Concepts of Analytical Psychology,* Princeton: Princeton University Press.

Wiesel, E. (1995) "Our Common Responsibility: Founder's Day Convocation Address," spoken at Bates College, Lewiston, Maine, on April 5, 1995; and also in C. MacDonald (1995) "Elie Wiesel: 'It is So Simple'," *Bates: The Alumni Magazine: Summer 1995.*

Wilbur, R. (2010) *Anterooms: New Poems and Translations*, Boston and New York: Houghton Mifflin Harcourt.

Willeford, W. (1987) *Feeling, Imagination, and the Self: Transformations of the Mother–Infant Relationship*, Evanston: Northwestern University Press.

Winnicott, D. W. (1965) "The development of the capacity for concern" in *The Maturational Processes and the Facilitating Environment,* London: Hogarth Press.

# Index

Page numbers shown in italic refer to an illustration.